MW00575754

SPORTSMAN'S
BEST

BOOK & DVD SERIES

FS Books:
Sportsman's Best: Inshore Fishing
Sportsman's Best: Offshore Fishing
Sportsman's Best: Snapper & Grouper
Sportsman's Best: Sailfish
Sportsman's Best: Trout
Sportsman's Best: Redfish
Sportsman's Best: Dolphin
Sportsman's Best: Snook
Sportsman's Best: Kayak Fishing
Sportsman's Best: Sight Fishing

Sport Fish of Florida
Sport Fish of the Gulf of Mexico
Sport Fish of the Atlantic
Sport Fish of Fresh Water
Sport Fish of the Pacific

Baits, Rigs & Tackle
Annual Fishing Planner
The Angler's Cookbook
Florida Sportsman Magazine

Florida Sportsman Fishing Charts
Lawsticks
Law Boatstickers
Field Guide
ID Lawsticks

Author, David A. Brown
Photo Credits, Alberto Knie, Joe Malat, Bill Varney, Pat Ford, Danno Wise,
Fred Brandt, Bob Haviland, David Gill, Mark Naumovitz, Jeff Weakley,
Gary Caputi, Steve Wozniak, Wade Hamamoto, Emily Bedsworth,
Kevin Blinkoff, Zach Frase, Lawrence Taylor, Marcus Heflin, David Thornton,
Mike Kennedy, Josh Ward, David Conway, David A. Brown
Edited by David Conway and Jeff Weakley
Graphic Design by Mark Naumovitz, Drew Wickstrom

ISBN-13: 978-1-934622-22-3
ISBN-10: 1-934622-22-2

www.floridasportsman.com

 Find us on
Facebook

SURF
FISHING

CONTENTS

SB

SPORTSMAN'S BEST
SURF FISHING

10

112

194

214

Foreword

Soul Surf Fisher

F ishing is a great, democratic sport—all who come can participate—and the surf is the common denominator of it all. To watch a surfcaster hurl his rig into that wild sea is a beautiful thing, as fine as a well-made fly cast or a well-thrown castnet. It's an action that speaks of generations of tradition and endurance and practice. To watch that surfcaster gingerly bring in a pompano or striped bass or drum—or any of the innumerable species that cruise our shores—that is a sight that many would also call quite fine.

David A. Brown has written a compelling, engaging tour of the surf fishing sport in America, and what a wonderful book it is. There is at every turn something to admire in these pages. The book is as much a travelogue of the places where surf meets sand and people fish as it is a guide and tipsheet to rigs, techniques and tactics. David A. Brown is one of the most traveled, experienced outdoors journalists in the country, and as this is his first book, we are glad to welcome him to the *Sportsman's Best Series*.

A veritable legion of surf fishing photographers assembled to contribute the hundreds of photos. Many of these photographers, like Alberto Knie, Joe Malat, Bill Varney, Pat Ford and Danno Wise, are expert anglers as well. They are the top, intrepid visual chroniclers of the sport in the country. Countless others contributed their photographs in the spirit of the sport itself—including Fred Brandt, Bob Haviland, David Gill, Mark Naumovitz, Jeff Weakley, Gary Caputi, Steve Wozniak, Wade Hamamoto, Emily Bedsworth, Kevin Blinkoff, Zach Frase, Lawrence Taylor, Marcus Heflin, David Thornton, Mike Kennedy, Josh Ward, myself and of course, the author, David A. Brown—all to create a book that truly represents our sport.

David Conway, Florida Sportsman Magazine

Sunsets like this add to the experience of surf fishing, and make it all the more worthwhile.

Alluring and accessible, the
surf offers an easy entry
point with room to expand.

Introduction
Why Surf Fishing

Ever shifting, ever changing; swirling and sweeping, it's realm rearranging. This is the surf—nature's gristmill, at the sea's doorstep. An intriguing premise in which the bounty of diverse opportunity meets straightforward simplicity and begs the question: "What are you waiting for?"

True, this is the ocean and standing face-to-face with all that aqueous real estate can at first seem overwhelming. However daunting it may be, this shared boundary of terra firma and the big brine may actually be the most welcoming and accessible zone of high potential in fishing's entirety. You need no boat, no vessel; no device of floating or propulsion. You can approach and depart as you please with fair expectation of finding the same scene upon your return.

Best of all, this is the ultimate congruence of relaxing leisure and focused intent – a true compromise for groups blending hardcore anglers with those of lesser commitment. So what if some enjoy their beach chairs and refreshments, while others watch rod tips like a bird dog on point? The surf does not judge.

In fact, knowledge, skill and interest tend to grow faster in such a comfortable environment devoid of demanding performance pressure. When it's time to move up the ladder, there's plenty of room to push yourself a little farther on each excursion. By comparison, plug casting for striped bass off the treacherous shores of New York's Montauk Point demands more from the surf angler than soaking shrimp for whiting off Florida's New Smyrna Beach. In between, a broad spectrum of enjoyable options can fill a lifetime.

For me, the surf has long held a nearly indescribable appeal. Maybe it's a simple fascination with the intricate ecosystems that start with the microscopic, progress to the little guys that tumble and burrow with each wave and expand to the big dudes that can make a 12-foot rod look like a willow branch. Could be that persistent inquisition keeps me wondering what lurks beneath each breaker. Whatever the narrative, combining the great unknown with personal proximity has always assured absolute angling alchemy.

One of my earliest saltwater fishing memories was a family beach weekend in Placida, Florida where chasing fiddler crabs somewhere below the high tide line proved delightful until we spotted a big fin cutting through the surf. Watching my uncle bait up the biggest fishing rod I'd ever seen with a chunk of mullet and fling that massive rig into the waves was pretty cool—but not nearly as cool as seeing that rod double over as line raced off the wailing reel.

Flash forward about a dozen years and I joined a high school buddy's family for a week in Boca Grande—famous for its summer tarpon bonanza, but also home to an active surf fishery. Here, in my last summer before departing my childhood home in Central Florida and moving to Tampa to attend USF, I'd catch my first snook in the surf, along with speckled trout, redfish and an awful lot of catfish.

Each night we walked a good mile to our favorite spot; all the way, trying in vain to catch the ghost crabs that startled us by scampering across the shell fragments. The hike was as much a part of that surf fishing adventure as those second-hand spinning outfits, that Ziploc bag of hooks and sinkers and that incredible feeling of warm waves slapping our knees as we kept watch for sharks and bet on whose rod was next to bend.

Since then, tumbling waves, salty breezes and that familiar tug of back-currents pulling against my ankles have lived in my heart like old friends that never drift too far away. Anyone who's known this fascination has heard the surf calling like seductive sea sirens beckoning Odysseus, though with far more benevolent intent.

Personal bonds are there for the making; available and indelible for young and old, novice or veteran. Some prefer fishing solo, while others enjoy group excursions. Each to his own, but capture the moments with lots of photos and video. Digital scrapbooks will remind you of treasured times past and motivate you to pay your old friends a visit now and then.

Get to know the surf and, like any great friendship, you'll find that the more time you spend learning its complexities and complements; its do's and its don'ts, the more deeply it will enrich your angling life with challenges and rewards aplenty. The waves are breaking and your next great moment is just a cast away, so the ocean asks: "What are you waiting for?"

David A. Brown, Author

CHAPTER 1

The Appeal

For our purposes, "surf fishing" will include beaches (sand and rocks), jetties and piers—basically, anywhere you can fish the ocean while standing on solid ground or some natural or manmade structure reachable on foot. From the get-go, let's banish the thought that a surf book holds any anti-boating implication. Actually, it's just the opposite. Fishing vessels of engine, paddle or poled propulsion offer many benefits of function and comfort that can greatly enhance your range of opportunities. In all likelihood, many who enjoy fishing from boats can trace some element of their initial angling interest to a shore-bound experience.

Surf fishing offers an easy entry point into the sport. No need to feel pressured; just learn at a relaxed pace.

An angler braves the treacherous rocks off Long Island for striped bass.

Big stripers reward anglers with thrilling fights and tasty filets.

The Surf Scene

The surf fishing experience ranges from the aggressive, risky jetty fishing action here . . .

Like any recreational activity, increasing interest, ability and budget may find surf anglers expanding their fishing operation to include something with a motor or a paddle. Conversely, it's no rarity to find boaters opting to "leave her in the slip" and just hit the beach now and then. Case in point: Mike Kennedy, my longtime friend from Mobile, Alabama hosted my first Northern Gulf offshore trip some 20-plus years ago. Today, he'll fire up the twin outboards when his family wants cobia or snapper for dinner, but he also spends a lot of time on the shores of Dauphin Island and the Florida Panhandle where pompano, redfish and whiting offer a nice balance to the offshore scene.

Surf fishing is but one of the many ways to enjoy the ocean's resources, but it's one that easily coexists with all others. In some instances, surf fishing hot spots sit detached from the mainland, so boating out to safe anchorage is the only option. From emergent shoals and sandbars off the Georgia Coast, to barrier islands like Anclote Key and Three Rooker Bar on Florida's Central Gulf Coast or Southern Cali-

. . . to casual sunset strolls along quiet, sandy beaches.

fornia's Channel Islands, great potential awaits those willing to make a short ride. For those who want to keep it simple, just head to the coast and find the nearest point of public access.

Introduce Beginners to the Sport

Even for adults, there's only so much information a person can absorb in one excursion. That's just not the case with surf fishing. If things get too heavy, just take a stroll down the beach and mentally unwind while taking in the relaxing scenery. Many surf anglers—experienced or otherwise—find a little sand castle construction profoundly therapeutic.)

Notably, learning to surf fish from an experienced angler is not the same thing as learning to surf fish like (read: "as good as") an experienced angler. When mentoring beginners, think baby steps. You don't teach someone to swim by marching them up to the high-dive platform and saying "jump." Hold off on the 12-foot rods and heavy rigs until your pupil gets a grip on the general concepts. Clearly, bigger targets require more substantial gear, but you can have a lot of fun with a 7-foot medium-action spinning outfit and for kids, a classic Zebco 33 spincast outfit beefed up with braided line will handle plenty of smaller species—particularly around the shallow ends of piers and jetties. Start them off at a level they can handle and when the big outfit bends, help your new angler support the rod while they crank the handle. Oaks grow from acorns.

From the beach, pier or jetty, surf fishing offers simple and convenient access to the ocean's bounty.

The excitement of being so close to the surf thrills young anglers.

The reward of a great catch like this pompano adds to the thrill.

Advantages of Surf Fishing

Surf fishing for pompano offers an affordable way to enjoy the sea's resources.

Economics

From subsistence fishing to personal recreation, the low-cost factor removes economic barriers. That's not to say a set of high-end surf outfits, top-shelf tackle and a decked-out, beach-friendly vehicle won't set you back a few paychecks, but the broad range of options keeps the game open to just about anyone who wants to play.

Several strategies will help you drive down the overall cost of your surf fishing activities. First, make friends at local tackle shops and join a fishing club with an emphasis on surf fishing. Get to know the insiders, gurus and beach bosses and you'll tap into the network of pre-owned, refurbished equipment, much of which has plenty of useful life remaining. Buy from someone who knows the sport and you'll be sure to start off with the right gear. Moreover, club members often share expenses for road trips to more distant surf fishing spots.

Also, frugal types know that keeping their natural baits chilled between uses extends their useful life and enables you to freeze the leftovers for future trips. Now, before the hate mail begins, fresh is always best so don't expect a frozen clam strip to bear the same appeal as those freshly shucked beauties. The same goes for frozen shrimp, sand fleas, finger mullet and just about any other natural baits you may use. However, between bites from the picky top-tier species, there's usually a plethora of B-teamers with far less discriminating palates that will keep the action rolling.

Two key advantages here: First, steady action is important for maintaining the interest of youth anglers or novices of any age. Second, feeding activity of any kind creates a buzz in the water—an intriguing mix of sight, sound and scent that serves as a living fish attractor for larger species. Especially relevant around piers, jetties and natural rock formations, getting the little guys buzzing will often attract attention from more desirable species that venture into your bait zone when they come to investigate the action.

Floating live baits in the shallow, clear surf is a good bet for Florida snook.

Socialization

Life is good when a hot bite leaves little time for talking, but with the variables of season, weather and daily ebb and flow come the inevitable slow periods. This is primetime for kicking back in the beach chairs, swapping stories, sharing laughs and taking those deep breaths of contentment that fill the heart and the lungs. Beaches have a way of loosening life's rigidity, dissipating stress and reminding us of how the simplest pleasures define happiness.

For those looking to advance their performance, local fishing clubs offer camaraderie and a great learning environment with members generally eager to promote the sport by teaching and encouraging others. These organizations also provide opportunities to volunteer for civic and benevolent events, as well as environmental stewardship efforts such as beach cleanups.

Spread the Joy

Logistical convenience facilitates tournaments and fun fishing days for underprivileged kids, disabled military veterans, and anyone in need of a little beachside R&R. Elsewhere, benevolent and spiritual outreach programs like Texas guide Marcus Heflin's Christian Surf Anglers specialize in teaching life lessons along with knots and casting technique.

A beaming smile and a nice black drum tell the memory-making story of an exciting day of Florida surf action.

Some beaches allow vehicle access, while others sit just a short stroll from public parking areas.

Plenty for All

Stand on the edge or wade right in—the surf offers options for all levels of skill and interest.

Carry what you need from your vehicle and you're fishing in no time.

U nlike bank fishing at the local pond or stream where excessive pressure might bring a downturn in productivity, the surf scene offers a greater system of replenishment—if for no other reason than the scope of fishable water available within walking distance. That being said, there are no endless resources. The ocean's inhabitants may enjoy the benefits of vast habitat, but harvesting too many of a spot's surf species, many of which are schoolers, can adversely affect the area.

This also rings true for bait sources, especially crustaceans and shellfish, which tend to be more site-specific than finfish, which migrate or at least roam their geographic regions. With bait and sport fish, adhering to local regulations on size, season and bag/possession limits should be the foregone conclusion, but don't max out just because you can. Practicing safe catch-and-release goes a long way toward maintaining the beach abundance.

Don't pass up the chance to surf fish for an hour or two before or after work or school.

Available and Flexible

Notwithstanding the prudence of proper planning, surf fishing favors spontaneity. Go on a moment's notice and, while operational readiness may vary, you could conceivably catch the same fish you would have caught after hours of preparation. Keeping a basic tackle bag in your vehicle and a couple rods and sand spikes by the door gives that spontaneity a boost, but don't pass up the chance to fish the surf for an hour or two before or after work, school or any other commitment. If you have an hour to kill—you can hit the beach, jetty or pier and stand a good chance of bending a rod.

It's All Connected

One of the great things about surf fishing is that many of the rigging and technique points, along with the where-to/when-to stuff will hold true no matter where you fish. The effects of currents, tide stage, sky conditions—the principles remain the same wherever you fish. Of course, regional variations are assumed, but once you learn how to tie a double dropper rig for Florida pompano, you'll have the basic formula for the high-low rig commonly used for croakers and trout in Virginia's surf. Coast-to-coast—the Carolina rigs that work for puppy drum off the coast of, well, North Carolina for example, will do just fine (in smaller form) if you want to catch surf perch off Southern California.

From Gulf Coast mackerel (above) to pompano on Florida's east coast, even a short trip to the surf can prove rewarding.

Learn the basics of rigging and fish behavior and you'll equip yourself for surf fishing in any region.

During a hot bite, like the pompano runs off South Florida, you won't lack for company.

Weather Less Hindering

When big winds push big waves, coastal and offshore fishing becomes less viable, while the churning water can actually enhance some aspects of surf fishing. Naturally, the sight-fishing game goes out the window, and you really don't want to be standing chest deep in heavy surf, or trying to maintain footing on a slick jetty or an isolated offshore rock when swamping waves threaten. But in terms of viability, surf anglers can get the job done in much worse conditions than their boating counterparts.

Moreover, when conditions deteriorate, packing up and walking back to your vehicle—even in whipping winds and driving rain—is far less worrisome than looking at a 20-mile homeward run through 6-foot seas. When skies clear, resuming a surf fishing mission is much easier and less time-consuming than re-launching a vessel and returning to the fishing grounds.

From jetty rocks, to sandy beaches, to a pier's elevated perch; surf fishing is remarkably weather-tolerant.

Even when the skies turn dim and the sea growls, surf anglers can still enjoy their sport.

When weather puts fish on the move, piers are places to catch them in transit.

Amazing Ambiance

Beaches inherently foster the feeling of seclusion and fulfill the urge to get away that we all feel at one time or another. On barrier island beaches like North Carolina's famed Outer Banks or Padre Island flanking the South Texas Coast, the sense of serene sanctuary requires little imagination. But even on fully developed beaches like those of Florida's southeast coast, turn your back to the condos, stare at the entrancing waves and it's amazing how quickly the hustle and bustle fades from consciousness.

Natural accents are many and they range from the statuesque to the living and breathing. In Georgia's Golden Isles Driftwood Beach at the north end of Jekyll Island boast the sea's wooden sculpture gallery, while sea stacks off the Oregon Coast guard pristine beaches like salty sentinels. Travel to North Carolina's Shackleford Banks or Assateague Island neighboring Maryland/Virginia's Chincoteague Bay and wild horses will keep you company—from a wary distance. Enhancing these memorable sites are seabirds, dolphins and all the many fascinating creatures that scamper, crawl, wriggle and dig amid sand, shell and rock.

Historical elements complement the mix, as coastal areas have long been sites of important structures from lighthouses, like North Carolina's famous collection, to the now-retired forts that once guarded inlets during times of war.

The visual beauty of fishing at the ocean's edge complements the action of reeling in fish.

A sunset (above) or a sunrise (below) adds to the ambient appeal of fishing in the surf.

Hook it and Cook it

A simple cooking grate and an open fire will yield unforgettable beachside meals.

The only thing better than catching a nice fish in the surf is preparing a fresh seafood dinner right next to the waters from which it came. If you're fishing in a state or local park, you might find sturdy metal grills handily available in the picnic area. (Great example: Fort Desoto Park at the north end of Florida's Tampa Bay.) Lacking such facilities, a propane camp stove or even a simple campfire with a cooking grate does just fine.

No matter how you prepare it, a fresh seafood meal always tastes better next to the ocean.

Species and preparations will vary by region, but whether you like your fish breaded and fried, pan seared in olive oil or steamed in a tent of heavy duty aluminum foil, there's something really special about cooking outdoors. And don't limit yourself to finfish. Where recreational oyster or clam harvest is allowed, a little mud work will deliver a bivalve bounty that's just right for a steam pot or roasting right over the hot coals of a driftwood fire. I've even had surf anglers tell me that they fish with plump market shrimp, so they can cook their leftover baits for dinner.

(Note: Since you're not on the water, you can fillet your catch right on the sand and enjoy a waterside shore dinner. However, not every beach allows open fires or any type of cooking operation, so check the local restrictions before commencing.)

Pack out all of your trash and if you fry food, let the used oil cool and then pour it into a sealable container for proper disposal. (Oil recyclers serving the restaurant industry typically accept

This angler filets his fresh catch by lantern light, while a cooler full of pompano and whiting promise someone a fine meal.

personal sized containers as well.) Also, avoid the temptation of tossing leftovers for the seagulls, crabs and any varmints living nearby. No doubt, the local cleanup crew will make short work of the free meal, but technically this can be considered littering, while feeding wildlife—especially in local, state or federal parks/refuges—is illegal.

A double header of pompano rewarded this surf angler's efforts.

Creature Comfort

Surf fishing surely has its extreme—long walks to distant beaches with no vehicular access, hazardous hikes on wave-swept jetties and the whole Montauk thing. In truth, the really adventurous stuff is actually a small piece of the pie. A more fitting description for the majority of beach, jetty and pier fishing would be "cool, casual and comfortable."

"Family-friendly" also fits, as blending a little fishing with the sunbathing, Frisbee tossing and waterside napping puts a whole new spin on this trip to the coast. (Just don't fall asleep with baits deployed or your rod may go for a swim.) Best thing about surf fishing is the motion; rather, the lack thereof. With your feet firmly planted on the beach or a solid structure, there's no equilibrium issues; thus no sea sickness. (To put it mildly, if you turn green while standing on land and just looking at the ocean, you're probably better suited for inland activities.)

Beautiful scenery and abundant wildlife complement the catching (and sometimes releasing) of surf fish.

Functional and family-friendly, modern piers often include weather shelters and restrooms.

The surf may turn rough, but from the beach, jetty or pier, the lack of motion prevents seasickness

Sharing those moments on the beach with children makes every surf fishing trip a success.

The young angler above enjoys inspecting the fish on his own time.

CHAPTER 2

Geography & Nature of the Spor

Order amid chaos, the surf may seem the ultimate contradiction, but there's actually a very clear pattern and process to where, when, and why fishing opportunity exists within this turbulent theater of sand, shell and sea life.

When calculating the benefit of fishing at the ocean's edge, consider that a football team's best defensive player is the sideline. Immovable and unavoidable, this separation of inbounds and out-of-bounds dictates the lateral extent to which any given play can reach. Defenders closing in on a ball carrier use the sideline as much as their tackling skills to limit yardage, while predators use the surf zone in much the same way by targeting prey in shallow water where limited space minimizes escape.

Surf fishing generally presents a low-impact activity, but know the risks and stay safe.

Whether you're fishing the California coast or casting for stripers off Montauk, the surf demands and deserves respect.

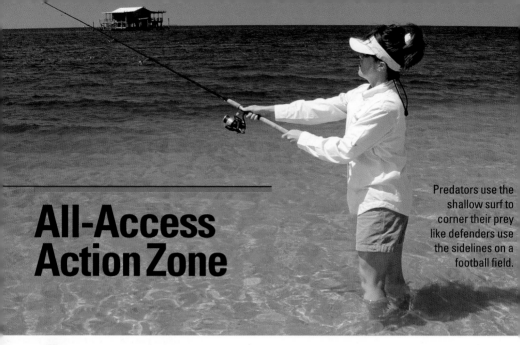

All-Access Action Zone

Predators use the shallow surf to corner their prey like defenders use the sidelines on a football field.

As a general rule, high tide affords predators—and anglers—the greatest opportunity, as it moves the fish closer to the beach. Conversely, low tide escorts the fish farther out. It may all seem relative—anglers simply follow the receding water line and adjust their game outward. However, because the ocean's bottom stays put even as the tide pulls water away, the actual playing field changes significantly with daily ebb and flow.

"Chasing the water," the strategy of incrementally moving outward to keep your baits in front of the fish, is doable but expect diminishing returns. This is especially true for regions like Georgia and lower South Carolina where the coast's southwestward slope creates a large tidal amplitude with daily fluctuations of 6 to 9 feet or more. Here, high incoming water is essentially the only viable option for surf anglers, as the fish are coming to the shallows, whereas an outgoing tide pulls the water out so far, so fast, that the fish tend to vacate as soon as they detect the ebb. You can still fish through a hard falling tide, but you'll spend more time setting and repositioning than fishing.

Be particularly careful about setting up at the end of a long outgoing tide. When the water turns, the rise can quickly overtake your position and in the best case scenario, you'll find yourself juggling an armful of rods, sand spikes and tackle while scrambling for higher ground.

The surf has key elements guiding and controlling the field of play, and you can use your understanding of them to be a better angler.

Gradually sloping low impact beaches spread the action over a broader surf zone.

Beaches

It may appear as simple as stand-on-the-sand, cast-into-the-water, but those seeking success beyond incidental catches will learn that there really is more to it than that. In terms of where to fish, think hills and valleys. The hills are sandbars formed by the stacking effect of wave action. Between these bars, the "guts" or "troughs" (valleys) are the surf's highways—distinct travel lanes for a variety of species. Some feed on the outer sloping edges, some like the bar tops, while others scavenge around in the troughs.

Following the wisdom of fishing near rocks and diving birds yielded a bent rod for this angler.

Breakers, those distinct lines of white water, occur when an incoming wave strikes the outer bar, rises overtop and tumbles back down on the nearshore side. The wave flattens through the adjacent trough as its volume spreads across the depth until the cycle reoccurs at subsequent bars until the energy reaches the beach and dissipates against the sand. High-impact beaches—those sharply angled toward the water—generally see a tighter and therefore more turbulent surf zone, whereas gradually sloping, low-impact beaches present a broader surf zone. In either case, wave action dislodges lots of crustaceans and other critters from the bottom, while knocking around baitfish and free-swimming crabs. Such vulnerable food sources give predators good cause to feed in the surf.

Any hard structure—natural or man-made—enhances the scene with additional habitat for forage and predators, along with current breaks that create eddies and ambush points. On Florida's Central Gulf Coast, Siesta Key's Point of Rocks Beach

Northeast Florida's Larry Finch travels the Atlantic Coast in search of fish and he's able to drive along many beaches to his spots.

finds a vein of flat limestone extending into the shallow surf, while farther up the coast, rubble from historic naval gun emplacements add structure to Fort Desoto Beach and nearby Egmont Key. Rocky coastlines like those lining much of the northeast and the Pacific Northwest bring plenty of additional elements to the surf scene.

Bait schools traversing the beach rarely go unnoticed by predators, so keep watch for "nervous water"—sections of the surface that seem to move contrary to or at least differently than, surrounding water. Also, dark shadows, bright glimmers of baitfish flashing, and any flipping or leaping are clear signs of a food parade. Train your eyes to look quickly at the face of a rising wave, as this brief "window" prior to the curl often reveals who's riding within.

Birds can also help you spot bait schools, so keep watch for ospreys, sea hawks and other birds of prey circling and diving talons-first at the water's surface. Pelicans crashing their pouched beaks into the waves, flying low to the water or sitting at the surface in large groups clearly signal bait in the area.

Birds can help you locate the bait schools that attract predators, so keep watch for gulls, terns, etc.

An early sunrise and calm conditions make prime fishing opportunities while walking the beach in hopes of sight fishing a snook.

Anglers casting into a calm, shallow surf should always keep watch for bait schools that attract predators.

This Maine angler makes his way through the dunes to access a low-impact beach.

Pompano are one of the top targets for pier anglers along most of the southern states.

When the bite's hot on a North Carolina pier, fishing spots fill up quickly.

Piers

A hybrid opportunity of elevation and extension, piers provide an emergent reef system with the added dimension of flowing water below. Piers boast additional benefits of shade in which forage and game fish often pass the heat of the day, along with lights, which create a whole different dynamic once the sun goes down. At night, baitfish and crustaceans are drawn to the light

Elevation, extension, shady undersides—piers offer surf anglers a menu of unique benefits.

things like moths to a street lamp. They become vulnerable to predators hiding in the peripheral shadows, waiting to ambush unsuspecting prey.

During daylight hours, the local food chain often puts on quite a show, as predators and prey engage in a high-stakes game of hide-and-seek. At times, it's just a quick glimpse of something big and shiny chasing something small and shiny through the waves. Other times, it's a straight-up food fest.

Case in point: One of the coolest images I recall from my early days of Gulf pier fishing was a dense school of cigar minnows that had surrounded the old Pensacola Pier. The water was black with baitfish, and each time a king or Spanish mackerel made a run at the chow line, the minnows in the immediate attack zone would leave a sudden hole in the dark sheet of living bodies, as they scrambled out of the way.

All the activity had not gone unnoticed by other pier patrons. A sudden flurry of frantic shouting and mad scramble saw no less than 20 surf rods whipping baits and plugs of various types into a surprisingly narrow zone. I dashed

Anglers await their next bite during a nice day on Florida's Juno Pier.

Pier anglers can expect to find a diverse mix of species all along the structure.

to the pier's end just in time to see a hammerhead shark—an honest 15-footer—slide past the crowd of pier regulars. The shark casually cruised some 30 yards down the beach, spun around and made a blistering run toward the outer edge of the bait/mackerel meat ball. One of the kings punched its ticket that day and the shark meandered offshore, completely oblivious to yet another round of overly optimistic casts.

Pier newcomers often grab their gear and make a bee line for the very end. That, in fact, could be the right move or the wrong, depending on A) what you want to catch, and B) how you picture your day proceeding. The larger species are generally more abundant near the deep water, but pier neophytes should understand that, while there are no officially reserved spaces, these structures usually see a distinct subculture of regulars who set up shop at the deep end and take their pursuits very seriously.

Rather than attempt to

muscle your way into their territory, best bet is to strike up a friendly conversation with one of the obvious pier elders. Ask how the gang likes to set up, what they're trying to catch and then state you interest in learning the drill. In most cases, a little courtesy will earn you not only acceptance, but invaluable instruction from the resident pier pros.

Keeper fish may roam from the first beach trough to well beyond the pier's end, while adjacent rock or rubble reefs are worth a few casts. Perimeter areas can certainly be productive, especially when bait schools

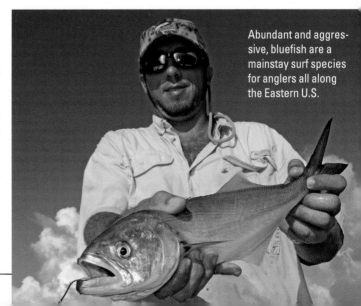

Abundant and aggressive, bluefish are a mainstay surf species for anglers all along the Eastern U.S.

hold nearby, but don't think that flinging your bait as far away from the pier as possible is the only option. Diversify your presentations by casting and retrieving a spoon, jig or diving plug parallel to the pier, or casting underneath and retrieving through the shaded waters. (Take care to avoid tangling other lines by surveying the area, checking for fellow anglers fishing the pier's other side directly behind you and giving anyone nearby the heads-up.) The general golden rule of pier fishing is: Cast straight out, perpendicular to the pier, from where you stand. When all anglers follow that rule, more people get to fish without unnecessary tangling of lines.

You'll also find opportunities by vertically dropping baits or hopping jigs near pilings—particularly those below a change in pier contour, such as a 'T' end. Pilings encrusted with barnacles, oysters and other sea growth present concentrated food sources for a variety of species. These centers of activity find the crustacean and shellfish lovers like redfish, black drum, sheepshead and spadefish investigating meal opportunities, while larger fish such as snook, cobia, snapper and jacks often pass by in hopes of picking off smaller forage species feeding on algae or seeking shelter in the shadows.

Piers with bait shops present a two-fold advantage: Obviously, it's handy to have access to replacement tackle and whatever baits you may be using. Additionally,

Pier veterans often stake out their spots at the end, but a little courtesy will earn newcomers a kinder welcome.

baitshops often dump the shrimp and baitfish that die in the live tanks over the railings. Nothing goes to waste in the ocean, so don't be surprised to spot some hefty fish lurking around these areas. Same goes for cleaning stations, and here's a tip: Fish scraps and carcasses that settle to the bottom attract lots of crabs, which in turn, attract predators with a taste for crustaceans. Fish a soft plastic crab imitation like Berkley's Gulp! baits on a light jighead and you might score big.

> **Pay particular attention to the pier's pilings, any contour changes and areas beneath cleaning boards and bait shop tanks.**

Jetties

Low tide allows access to the jetty's perimeter, but this angler will eventually have to move higher onto the rocks when the water rises.

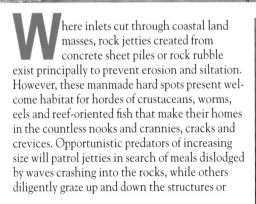

Different fish species hang out at different depths along a jetty. Don't neglect the shallows.

Where inlets cut through coastal land masses, rock jetties created from concrete sheet piles or rock rubble exist principally to prevent erosion and siltation. However, these manmade hard spots present welcome habitat for hordes of crustaceans, worms, eels and reef-oriented fish that make their homes in the countless nooks and crannies, cracks and crevices. Opportunistic predators of increasing size will patrol jetties in search of meals dislodged by waves crashing into the rocks, while others diligently graze up and down the structures or utilize the rocks for their own ambush feeding.

Jetties, like piers, extend an angler's reach far beyond the beach; and while high tides give predators maximum access to the structure's beach side, the inlet side and the seaward end can prolong the fishing opportunities long after an outgoing tide has drained the beach. Look for features that stand out from the rest of the jetty, such as flares and points along the edges and breaks in the structure where tides wash through. These contour changes create feeding points for the fish you seek.

Some jetties like Florida's Sebastian inlet and

those at Surfside, Texas include paved surfaces, which offer safe and convenient passage, while others present a walk-at-your-own-risk scenario. It's no secret that the spots hardest-to-reach can offer homerun potential, but the risk-reward equation cannot be overstated and should not be overlooked. Be smart and let your spouse or a trusted contact know where you'll be fishing and when you expect to return. Taking a moment to

New England's trophy striper specialist Alberto Knie unhooks a big cow.

For optimal jetty fishing results, look for points, breaks and any other fish-attracting features.

outline where you'll go, what time you intend to leave and return, who's going with you (solo trips on long jetties are ill-advised) and what you're wearing will provide potentially life-saving information should the unthinkable occur.

Throughout the surf zone, some anglers like calm water, while others want it roiling and churning. Some of this decision is based on local species and habit. For example, rough water can ignite a mean northeast striper bite. On the other hand, trout and redfish anglers in the northern Gulf of Mexico and snook anglers targeting the linesider's summer spawning aggregations on both sides of the Florida peninsula prefer calmer conditions for sight fishing.

Spring through mid-fall (basically, the Easter-to-Thanksgiving period) will keep you in the ballpark for most regions. Water temperature typically guides baitfish migrations like fall mullet runs along the East Coast and the Gulf of Mexico. Tune into fishing reports up the line, to keep current on the progressions, as predators follow their appetites. Cooling

Florida's John Carpenter displays one of the flounder he caught on live finger mullet near the Ponce Inlet jetty.

Understanding your region's species mix and their seasonal migrations or movements will help you dial in an effective surf-fishing plan.

Wave action creates a pocket of opportunity between the beach and the Ponce Inlet north jetty.

waters will also push migrating gamefish, from pompano to mackerel and many others, toward southern wintering grounds, with the process reversing during the spring warm up.

Common surf species from New England through the Mid-Atlantic include striped bass, bluefish, flounder, weakfish and sharks. The Carolinas through Georgia see a lot of redfish, tarpon, sharks, black drum, sheepshead, weakfish, whiting, spot, bluefish, stripers, pompano and sharks. Florida's east coast attracts a similar mix as its northern neighbors, but weakfish, spots and blues become less frequent, while the subtropical bonefish and permit accent the southern surf zones.

Gulf state surf anglers love their redfish, speckled trout and flounder, but pompano, whiting, silver trout, mackerel, jack crevalle, bonito and sharks keep things lively. Florida and South Texas also boast loads of snook, while surf perch, spotfin and yellow croakers, cabezon, California halibut, leopard sharks, corbina and stripers keep California anglers busy.

Year-to-year, the seasonal assortments are fairly predictable, but the occasional oddball keeps things interesting. For example, from Florida's southwest coast to about Maryland, warmer months bring plenty of opportunity for surf anglers to tug on bull, blacktip, bonnethead and tiger sharks. Suffice it to say that pulling a big thresher or tiger shark onto the sand earns an angler several weeks of bragging rights. Giant stingrays (aka "mud marlin"), while hardly a glamorous species, are always a crowd-maker. Releasing these big catches not only helps the fish populations, but scores some P.R. points from curious onlookers.

Amid the usual mix of surf species, the occasional oddball like a big shark or giant stingray never fails to liven up the scene.

Beware the Hazards

I n many cases, surf fishing brings no more risk than a walk on the beach or a dip in the waves, but don't let the sport's generally low-impact vibe lull you into a false sense of security. Anytime you handle sharp objects (your tackle and sometimes your quarry's teeth and spines), it's wise to stay alert and avoid mishaps. That part's pretty simple, but what complicates matters is the habitat in which surf fishing occurs. Describing the fun without noting the potential hazards would be a disservice, so just consider these areas of concern and then let forethought serve your protection.

Don't let a calm surf fool you. Jetty fishing remains a risky option in many conditions.

reaches. If there's no such demarcation, there's a good chance the jetty end submerges at high tide, or constant wave action keeps it essentially covered. You do not want to let a tide sneak up

Traversing Unpaved Jetties

With daily wave washing, some of the rocks you'll traverse can be very slippery with moisture and algae. Wet rocks typically appear darker than dry ones, while brighter coloration (reds, greens) indicates sea growth that can feel like oil on ice. Suddenly losing traction and balance over an unforgiving terrain can deliver a painful fall, or a tumble into deep and often turbulent water.

Bait schools gathering near jetties bring a high level of opportunity, but don't let the excitement diminish your caution.

If you're new to the jetties, scout the area (in person or online), know the tide schedule for your fishing day and pay attention to high-tide marks—actual salt lines, dried weeds, flotsam, etc. —that will indicate how high the water

on you, especially if the jetty holds a dip or low spot between your position and the shallow end. Currents rip through these spots and ill-timed crossings can quickly take a turn for the tragic.

Surf fishing certainly has its share of hazards, but alertness and caution will help ensure a safe experience.

After Hours

Night fishing can be hugely successful, especially during summer, but note the risks that come with decreased visibility. Sharks and stingrays, jellyfish, sharp objects, other fishing lines—many hazards easily avoided during the day can go undetected in low light. Nighttime jetty fishing requires utmost attention to footing, gear placement and tide progress. You won't notice tide levels as easily as you will during daylight, so headlamps, waterproof lanterns or flashlights with lanyards are essential gear for night missions here and anywhere you fish the surf.

Weather Windows

High winds and even rain may be tolerable on the beach or pier, but jetty anglers must consider the decreased stability and the potential for lost gear. If foul weather traps you on a jetty, tuck your gear into a reachable crevice and tuck in close to a shielding rock on the downwind side until the danger passes.

In the south particularly, summer storms bring a sudden drop in barometric pressure and a cooling downdraft, which can stimulate incredible, aggressive feeding among coastal species. The window of opportunity is brief and intense, but don't push too far. Once the low rumbling turns to sharp claps of intense thunder, lightning is well inside your safe zone. Actually, lightning can deliver deadly strikes from up to 10 miles away. No fish is worth such risks, so know your limits and pack it up when the sky turns angry.

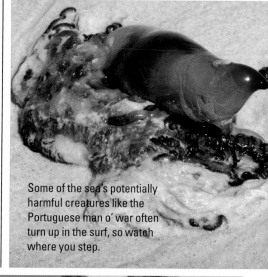

Some of the sea's potentially harmful creatures like the Portuguese man o' war often turn up in the surf, so watch where you step.

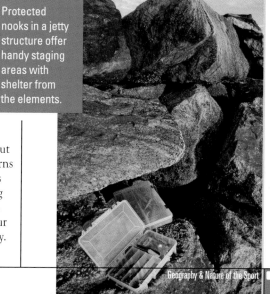

Protected nooks in a jetty structure offer handy staging areas with shelter from the elements.

Don't Go With the Flow

When water from breaking waves returns to the sea by running roughly perpendicular to the coast, usually through a cut in the sand bar, the strong channelized flow creates a rip current running contrary to the surf. Rip currents present not only a profound physical risk, but also a psychological challenge, as panic limits one's ability to take prudent action. Understand that while certainly dangerous, rip currents are usually manageable if you keep cool and take evasive action. Attempting to fight your way through a rip current leads to exhaustion, but swimming parallel to the shore minimizes exertion and eventually leads you to calmer water where you can start to angle yourself back toward shore. (For information on rip currents, visit www.ripcurrents.noaa.gov)

When wading above your knees, particularly on slick jetties or natural rocks, a lightweight personal flotation device (PFD) belt pack provides peace of mind without limiting your range of motion. Use the ripcord models, rather than water-activated or you can plan on inadvertent wave inflations. Likewise, a throwable floatation device is a smart accessory for jetty fishing.

Distinct run-outs often signal the potential for dangerous rip currents.

Fact Box: 30/30 Rule for Lightning Safety

Any lightning safety plan should incorporate the 30/30 Rule. The 30/30 Rule states that people should seek shelter if the "Flash-To-Bang" delay (length of time in seconds between a lightning flash and its subsequent thunder) is 30 seconds or less, and that they remain under cover until 30 minutes after the final clap of thunder.

A 30-second lead time is necessary prior to a storm's arrival because of the possibility of distant strikes. A 30-minute wait after the last thunder is heard is necessary because the trailing storm clouds still carry a lingering charge. This charge can and does occasionally produce lightning on the back edge of a storm, several minutes after the rain has ended.

Studies have shown most people struck by lightning are struck not at the height of a thunderstorm, but before and after the storm has peaked. This shows many people are unaware of how far lightning can strike from its parent thunderstorm. DO NOT wait for the rain to start before seeking shelter, and do not leave shelter just because the rain has ended.

- From the National Weather Service

Feeding Frenzies

Bait schools passing through the surf almost always have catchable predator fish following them, but if a pod of sardines, mullet or bunker swings into the area you're wading you could find yourself right in the middle of a briny buffet when the sharks close in for a feed. The sharks rarely have any interest in humans—we're just in their way some of the time. However, when the chewing starts, the water turns to a bloody, scaly froth and visibility drops to nearly nothing. Sharks are usually biting blind in a mad rush to grab something edible, so you just don't want to be the unintended victim of mistaken identity. The moment you find yourself surrounded by baitfish—especially if they're tightly bunched and clearly nervous—simply walk backward toward the beach and keep your rod butt facing forward in case anyone needs a redirecting nudge.

These Long Island anglers are doing their best to take advantage of a feeding frenzy happening close to their rocky platforms.

With all of these points, the intent is not to dissuade surf fishing interest with thoughts of tragedy. Rather, security through awareness ensures a safe and enjoyable day of uninterrupted fishing.

The striper blitz off Montauk, Long Island is one of the best-known surf fishing opportunities in the entire country.

CHAPTER 3

Tackle Options

One of the most welcoming aspects of surf fishing is the low-cost entry point, which presents no financial barrier for beginners and casual enthusiasts. Even the frequent surf angler will enjoy plenty of success with rod-reel combos that come in well below the $100 mark. But like any pursuit, surf fishing tackle selection comes down to the right tool for the job. You can go as specific as your budget allows and within today's mosaic of modern tackle technology, you can usually find the rod and reel that suits your intentions.

Just start with what your budget allows and expand as your interest grows.

Gear up appropriately for your chosen surf fishing activity. Above, an angler uses low tide to his advantage to fly fish near a jetty in Maine.

Smooth Operator

Exposure to sand, salty air and the occasional wave can take a toll on gear. Regular maintenance helps keep your reels in good condition.

Cleaning rods and reels after each saltwater exposure helps keep your gear functioning properly. That's important, but you'll improve overall performance—particularly casting distance—with lubrication treatments. Short-range presentations like flounder fishing casts from a North Carolina pier, or tossing light rigs for California surf perch rarely need more than a gentle lob; but when you really need to punch a bait way out there—over shoreline rocks, or past a gradually sloping bottom—you'll appreciate anything that facilities "smooth" and "far."

Keep your tackle in top operating condition and it will serve you well.

Checking/adding reel grease is a simple maintenance step for do-it-yourselfers, but reel service centers can handle such things during routine cleanings. The manufacturer's standard lubricant will keep things moving as they should, but Massachusetts surf pro and 5-time U.S. National Casting Champion Ron Arra offers these tips for achieving maximum casting distance with conventional reels (the common choice for long-casters):

"I clean out the manufacturer's grease in the bearings and replace it with 20-weight 3-in-1 oil," Arra said. "In the wintertime you want 10-weight. The less oil in the bearings the better, but you have to remove the bearings from the reel and clean them by letting them soak in lighter fluid. Do this maybe once a month, depending on how much you fish.

"If you're fishing every day, then you put one drop of oil in each bearing three times a week. It's good to heat up the bearing as hot as you can with a hair dryer, because then the oil will go right inside the bearing."

Several lubrication products offer performance enhancing and corrosion-resistance properties that can help optimize your tackle performance and extend its useful life. Examples include Quantum's Hot Sauce, Blakemore Reel Magic, Abu-Garcia Silicote Reel Lube, Penn Reel Lube and Cleaner and TG's Rocket Fuel. DYNA-TEK offers a Rod & Reel Performance Kit that features a nonstick flexible nano-ceramic coating, which reduces friction and vibration between the rod, guides, line and reel. Doing so reduces line drag and maximizes casting distance. The clear coating also protects against corrosion and dirt or ice buildup. The Fishing Performance Kit includes towelettes with Rod & Guide Coat, Reel & Line Coat, Ceramic Treatment Coat and Alcohol Cleaner. (DYNA-TEK.com). In addition to alcohol, Arra said lighter fluid makes a good cleaning agent for reel components.

Keeping it Together

When carrying multiple rods—perhaps 2-piece models broken down—you can quickly find yourself wrestling with lots of pieces going every which way but where you want them. Eliminate the headache and minimize the risk of damage by tethering each set of rod pieces, and then secure the bundle as a whole.

Zip ties are one way to go, but the cost factor of a single-use item bears consideration. Rubber bands or elastic hair bands provide longer life at a lower cost (buy in bulk), but keep several backups handy, as exposure to heat and saltwater will eventually cause breakage. Pipe cleaners also work, but in time, the twisting and untwisting will weaken the wire.

For gathering a group of rods, a simple piece of cloth cord will do the trick and with loops tied at each end, you can run one loop through the other for a quick cinching job that leaves a carrying handle. Hook-and-loop products offer a handy option for large or small gather-

Creativity and ingenuity yield several rod-binding options.

ings. Velcro makes an adjustable marine grade straps that'll bundle several rods and stand up to the saltwater environment.

Industrious types can fashion a slip-on rod binder from the versatile pool noodle. Cut inch-wide discs off the noodle's end, drill a center hole just wide enough to accommodate the rods you intend to secure (multiple single-piece rods or broken down 2-piece models) and then cut a radial slit in one side of the disc. Slip the rods (or rod pieces) through the slit and position the foam disc so it fits snugly.

Fishing Butler simplifies the whole deal with a flexible loop fitted with an adjustable, locking buckle that snugs against rods with a non-abrasive surface and opens with a quick-release tab. Just fit the loop over whatever rod grouping you need to secure, slide the buck toward the rods to tighten the loop and then release the buckle's locking tab to slide open (See fishingbutler.com).

Many budget-friendly rods like Shakespeare's Powerod lineup offer economical entry-level options.

Transporting surf fishing rods can be a delicate operation, but fastening rods into manageable bundles facilitates the effort.

Cast Away

Reel manufacturers like Penn, Shimano, Daiwa, Abu-Garcia, and Quantum/Fin-Nor offer models developed with surf fishing in mind and most anglers will find a good range of products for any budget. Those who demand a higher level of performance may opt for a custom tuning package from reel specialists like long distance tournament caster Ryan White of North Carolina's Hatteras Jack tackle shop (HatterasJack.com). For maximum distance and optimal casting control, White tricks out most any modern reel with improvements such as adjustable magnetic brake systems, carbon fiber drag washers, performance handles and more durable ceramic bearings (to replace stainless steel bearings).

Now, except for the ranks of hardcore surf-fishing devotees, where the revolving spool reel's superior casting distance holds rank, personal preference guides the choice of spinning or conventional/baitcasting gear. Spinning reel are the most user-friendly because line leaves the spool in self-regulating wraps, as opposed to the direct course of a revolving spool reel. Because of this, revolving spool reels are prone to overrun ("backlashing," "birds nest")—especially with braided line, so beginners usually learn their basic casting mechanics on spinning gear and then expand their reel repertoire when they're ready for more control and performance.

Spinning reels also allow you to mount the handle on either side—a big benefit for left-handed anglers. On the other hand (no pun intended) spinning reels are subject to the line-twisting scourge of "reeling against the drag"—turning the handle when a fish is running. Also, spinners can develop spool loops when a wrap enters the spool loosely and subsequent wraps trap the errant line. Eventually, that wayward loop will exit the spool during a cast and snarl your line.

High-end gear facilitates success, but anyone can learn to surf fish with a basic budget priced outfit.

A conventional reel's revolving spool, like this Akios reel's, calls for thumb control to manage the line during a cast.

At left, spinning gear is more beginner-friendly. Below, the propensity for overruns ("backlashing") makes conventional gear more challenging.

Advanced surf fishermen often prefer conventional reels.

Tip: If you notice a loop on your spinning reel, resist the urge to open the bail and peel off line. At some point, that loop will jump off the spool, tangle with the line ahead of it and create an exasperating snarl. The simplest way to clear a spinning reel loop is to keep the bail closed, loosen your drag and slowly pull line off the reel until the loop emerges. The closed bail keeps the line under control and prevents tangles.

For casting accuracy and efficiency, conventional/baitcasting reels stand superior, whether it's foot-long poppers thrown for trophy striped bass, or 4-inch suspending baits for speckled trout. Also, long casts with conventional reels are easier on the fingers, as line control simply requires adjusted thumb pressure.

By comparison, a spinning reel cast begins with your finger (typically the index) holding the line snug against the rod, with the bail open. As you cast, extending your finger releases the tension and allows line to exit the spool. Considering the force generated by a long surf road loading up and propelling a heavy bait rig (or plug), the line zips off your finger at a blistering speed. Cold weather and braided line intensify the discomfort and leave you with a sore trigger finger.

Florida surf angler David Gill prefers his spinning tackle but hates the line burn hazard.

He lessens the burden by tightening his drag before he casts, thereby maximizing line tension. The taught line snaps off his index finger more cleanly, as opposed to the sliding (thereby burning) motion of a line with "play."

Slip-on finger guards or waterproof Flexx-Wrap (Thesurfcaster.com) can further alleviate the discomfort. Another option: The index finger from a rubber fishing glove will also do the job. To prevent loss between uses, punch a hole (no slits, which can continue tearing) near the bottom edge of the finger guard and fashion a simple wrist strap with heavy monofilament. Use a loop knot for a non-cinching connection to the finger guard and an adjustable loop for your wrist.

For maximum finger protection, the Breakaway Canon (Breakaway.com) mounts to the handle of a spinning reel, holds the line with a clamping arm (as your index finger would) and uses a trigger mechanism to free the line for a cast. Functioning much like an archery release, the Canon prevents casting cuts by eliminating finger contact.

When selecting your surf reel, understand the pros and cons of conventional vs. spinning.

Gear Box

For those who clean, tweak and tune their own reels, writer Jeff Holder released a helpful guidebook of basic reel maintenance for baitcasting and spinning reels. Holder's *Fishing Reel Care and Maintenance 101*, from Piscator Publishing, guides anglers through the work with simple instructions and basic color pictures. Special sections are devoted to popular reels, and a DVD is included with more than 8,600 reel schematics and 1,900 manuals and guides. The book sells for $24.95. For more info, see www.reelschematic.com.

While Florida has some of the best surf fishing in the States, North Carolina—with the long distances out to the troughs from the beach—has some of the country's best surfcasters. So you'll find some expert sources of information on improving your casting gear coming from North Carolina. The folks at Hatteras Jack sell an extensive list of parts needed to improve reel performance. See their Web site, www.hatterasjack.com . Also, check out www.Hatterasoutfitters.com.

In Europe, distance casting is its own sport with a strong following of enthusiasts. An English company, Rocketfuel, makes reel bearings, spools and a lubricant to juice your casting distance. Their Web site has plenty to say about improving reel performance. See www.therocketreelcompany.com.

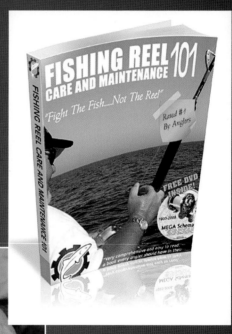

With the levelwind guide removed for speed, mount in reel body needs a protective cover.

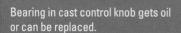

Bearing in cast control knob gets oil or can be replaced.

Hot Rod Reels

Surfcasting for distance? Spinning reels work
[fi]ne, and may be a better choice for anglers
[m]ore familiar with that gear, but there's always
[go]ing to be the slight friction of the line whip-
[pi]ng off the spool and the nagging sense of
[co]mpromised distance. Conventional reels by
[de]sign suffer no friction of the line against the
[sp]ool. Only the speed of the spool's spin ham-
[pe]rs the release and the distance achieved.

The smoothest and freest-spinning spool is the
[ul]timate objective of long-distance casters. Even
[w]ith good equipment, you can tweak your reels to
[ge]t improved distance out of your throws.

First off, maintain a strict cleaning and tuning
[re]gimen for their reels—the ground rules of
[go]od performance. That entails a mineral spirits
[b]ath to remove heavy grease from reel parts, fol-
[lo]wed by a bath of ultrasonic cleaner.

Some dedicated casting reels are made
[w]ithout levelwind guides. If yours has one, you
[c]an remove it to decrease friction and to speed
[th]e reel's rotation. If you do, remember to take
[o]ut the gear that controls it, too. To protect the
[re]el's interior from salt, you must cover the open
[m]ount in the reel's body for the levelwind shaft
[w]ith a form-made plastic insert. Aluminum air
[co]nditioning tape also covers those gaps.

Reels possess either centrifugal brake blocks or
[m]agnetic brake systems, both of which can be ad-
[ju]sted for either greater or lesser spool resistance.
[U]pper-echelon reels with magnetic brake systems
[a]re designed and geared for surfcasting right out
[o]f the box, and require no basic modifications for
[ex]cellent performance. Of course, that doesn't
[st]op enthusiasts from tinkering with them.

Free-flowing bearings are the really impor-
[ta]nt keys to getting casting distance. You can
[p]ut ceramic bearings
[i]n there for super
[sp]eed, but most guys
[w]ill take the [stock]
[b]earings out, take
[t]he dust covers off
[a]nd throw them away,
[c]lean the bearings and put a lightweight oil,
[li]ke Reel Power RP-10, in there.

Long-distance casting devotees use high-speed
[lu]bricants as a matter of course. Some of the best
[k]nown high-speed reel oils include TG's Rocket
[F]uel, Quantum Hot Sauce Reel Lube and Speed-
[X]. (See Smooth Operator, page 42).

In terms of casting
smoothness, conventional
reels (above) typically outpace
spinning gear (below).

Spooling Up

Monofilament an
braid both hav
their benefits, s
make sure yo
understand wha
best suits you
purpose

When choosing your line, consider that the way monofilament stretches works well for casting heavy natural bait rigs, as the inherent "give" helps prevent ripping hooks from their bait. Conversely, braided lines offer superior strength and sensitivity/response for working artificials. Braid's thinner diameter (relative to its breaking strength) enables you to carry more yardage on your spool—helpful if you tie into a big fish with sprinting ability.

Consider that braided line costs much more than monofilament of comparable breaking strength, while its thinner diameter means your reel will hold more braid than mono. Sticker shock awaits uninformed anglers who drop off a reel with instructions to "fill it up with braid," but filling part of your spool with monofilament backing moderates the cost. Mono also prevents slippage—the common vexation of tying braid directly to a spool.

The International Gamefish Association (IGFA.org) offers a formula for estimating how much mono backing you'll need; but everyone has their comfort level, so factor your intended use with the budgetary considerations. Some anglers forego backing on smaller capacity spools, while those targeting big fish may bite the bullet and go all-in with a big spool packed with braid. In any case, you'll need at least a few wraps of mono, or a rubber band to provide your braid with a gripping point. Some of today's modern reels, like Fin-Nor Lethal series include a rubber braid band on the spool to allow direct spooling sans the slippage.

Depending on spool size and your backing quantity, some of your braid may never see the light of day. When the top end starts showing signs of wear, maximize your investment by tying that older braid to new backing on another reel and winding it onto the new spool. "Flipping" your braid brings the new end to the forefront and avoids the cost of new line.

When spooling with braided line, you'll usually need monofilament backing to prevent slippage.

With either option, high-visibility line helps you keep track of your angles and helps prevent adjacent lines from tangling. Also, with any line choice, fluorocarbon leaders are usually a good idea for the added strength, abrasion resistance and a nearly-invisible presence. In clear, calm surf, wary fish will spot braided line, so fluorocarbon saves you from spooking fish. Additionally, fluoro makes a much better handle than the thinner braid—a benefit you'll appreciate when you're trying to land a big fish over rocks or haul a heavy catch out of the surf.

Regarding spool capacity, the surf species that

will actually "take drag" (pull out additional line) are less common than those you'll wind in fairly quickly. Nevertheless, jumbo red drum frequently pick up pompano baits and big stingrays will vacuum up whatever they find, so just make sure you're geared-up for not only your target species, but whatever else might also wander through the area. Anglers wading a western Louisiana beach for trout, or walking the Florida shores for snook seldom require more than medium to medium-heavy spinning or baitcasting outfits with line capacities of about 150 yards. However, when you throw a piece of meat into the surf, you'd better have at least 300 yards of line on that reel or you might find out how well you tied that spool knot.

Rod Ready

Generally speaking, the surf's unpredictable species mix makes it better to have too much rod than too little, as long as it does not impede your style of fishing. For example, anglers along the upper Texas coast may deploy large baits for sharks and bull redfish on 10- to 12-foot rods with hefty reels, but between the big bites, they'll wade the surf and cast to trout, flounder and smaller reds with 7-foot medium-action spinning or baitcasting outfits. In simplest terms, longer rods allow you to reach out and over breaking waves or shoreline rocks to place a bait or lure where the fish are feeding. Conversely, shorter rods are better for close-range casting, light tackle bait fishing (i.e. California surf perch) and most wading scenarios.

For maximum performance with minimal fatigue, pick a rod that you're comfortable casting, but consider what you'll be throwing and where you'll be throwing it. A surf rod's "action"—es-

Since you never know what will bite, it's usually better to have too much rod than too little.

sentially, how far down the blank it bends when loaded by bait or lure weight—greatly influences casting effort and distance. A "fast" action rod bends closer to the tip, while a rod with slow action bends all the way to the butt section with what's often called a "parabolic curve."

Again, model selection boils down to personal preference, but a few key points merit consideration. Stiffer, fast-action rods are best for launching lures great distances over rocks or big breakers, while providing the sensitivity to work artificials, along with the power to set the hook from afar. At the other end of the spectrum, slower parabolic rods absorb much of this sensitivity and punch, but they require less heaving effort. Moreover, they offer a softer delivery with less chance of ripping hooks from natural baits on the cast.

High-end custom rods may combine the best of both worlds, with generous flexibility buttressed by the strength necessary to handle a big fish. Such hybrid models really shine in scenarios where anglers work in tight spaces. As Long Island angler Craig Cantelmo points out, open beaches allow you to land a fish by simply walking backward and dragging it ashore, while isolated perches such as jetties or the outer rocks off Montauk Point present more challenging scenarios.

"Imagine a 30-pound striped bass swimming around your rock and you're trying to

Travel surf rods typically break down into two pieces, but experts like one-piece rods for the action (right).

Different rod actions are designed for particular performance benefits so choose the one that does what you need it to do.

or party stores) strapped to the rod tip with zip ties. Make sure you're aware of any state or local ordinances restricting the number of fishing rods in use.

Left and below, these anglers clearly enjoyed the results of using the right rod for their fishing style.

grab the leader on an 11-foot rod," Cantelmo said. "If you're standing on a rock and you're trying to land a big fish, you have to reach out and grab the leader. By doing so, you're lifting the rod in a very dangerous position. You essentially have to 'high stick' every time you land a fish, making a more parabolic rod important so you don't snap the tips off rods."

With any rod selection, you'll optimize performance by adhering to the specs printed on the blank. Even entry level rods are built to perform best with the specified line and weight range.

On a practical note, natural bait fishermen setting multiple lines should stagger their rods to prevent tangled lines, while keeping everything within easy reach. Monitoring is best done from one end of your rod set, as standing in the middle keeps you looking back and forth and doubles your effort. Non-daylight hours make it tough to spot strikes, so for multi-rod spreads, consider a signaling device such as a clip-on bell or a thin light stick (Walmart

An important consideration for your rod purchase is the grip—its shape, fit, feel and material. The Shimano Tiralejo here has a narrow-diameter, grippy butt and handle to help whip out the cast.

Tackle Storage

Simplicity buoys surf fishing's popularity and, while a simple Ziploc bag may handle enough hooks, swivels and sinkers for those casual beach days, tackle container selection should advance according to one's interest level. Most tackle shops and online retailers have a viable product for any budget, but basic features to look for include a sturdy rubber base that can sit on wet sand, waterproof or at least water-resistant material, padded shoulder strap and plastic or stainless steel zippers. Buy a cheap bag with basic metal zippers and saltwater corrosion will cause them to seize up in short order—before eventually falling apart.

Saltwater intrusion is nearly unavoidable, especially when fishing right next to it. However, modern designs like Plano's Hydro-Flo Bags (Planomolding.com) and

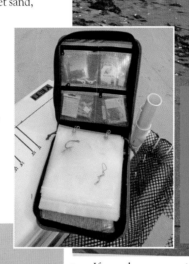

Natural bait anglers are wise to stagger their lines to minimize tangles. (Inset) Soft sided rig bags keep various tackle configurations at close reach.

Bags with water-resistant covers and flow-through bottoms help protect your tackle.

Shimano's Bluewave Surf Bag are made with water resistant covers and flow-through bottoms. With any tackle bag, rinse all your tackle with fresh water and let the tray stand in the sunlight long enough to dry. If you're in a hurry, hit the tray with a hair dryer to accelerate the process. For ongoing protection, a light dusting of talcum powder keeps corrosion at bay.

If you plan on camping out on a particular location and working from a beach cart or tailgate (when vehicles are allowed on the beach), tackle bag needs are less technical. However, for long wading missions, or tedious hikes onto the jetties, less is more. A heavy load of gear hastens fatigue and limits mobility—a safety issue, as much as an operational concern. And if you sit a tackle bag down to work a big fish, you may return to find it's been confiscated by waves or sticky fingers.

Think about what your style of fishing actually needs and match your tackle bag to a reasonable amount of these items. Example: For walking rocky northeast shores, renowned trophy striper hunter "Crazy" Alberto Knie designed the Tactical Anglers Assault Pouch—a 7- by 5-inch container for bucktails, softbaits and terminal tackle with quick-access Velcro cover and drain holes (Tacticalanglers.com). For hard baits, the Striper Lure/Plug Bag (TackleUS.com) stores up to 10 baits vertically in tangle-free plastic tubes.

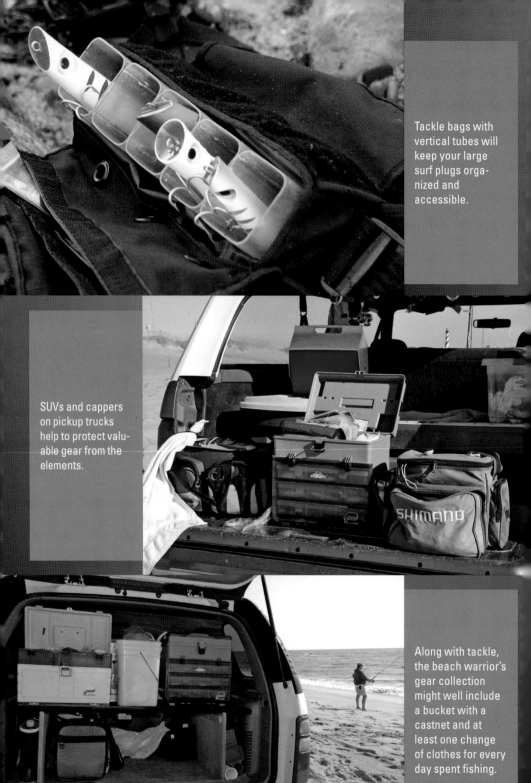

Tackle bags with vertical tubes will keep your large surf plugs organized and accessible.

SUVs and cappers on pickup trucks help to protect valuable gear from the elements.

Along with tackle, the beach warrior's gear collection might well include a bucket with a castnet and at least one change of clothes for every day spent fishing.

Vehicle-mounted rod and gear racks, here and right, make it easy to transport equipment to the beach and drive-on piers like Florida's Sunshine Skyway Fishing Piers (center).

The power of your livewell pump (and battery) must increase with the size of your well.

Where vehicle access is permitted, the ability to drive right up to the surf greatly expands your mobility.

Bed-mounted rod racks can be made at home with PVC, while aluminum models are sold at surf tackle stores.

CHAPTER 4

The Right Apparel

Comfort, safety and protection against the elements—that's the basic formula for selecting your surf-fishing apparel. Only a handful of scenarios, like traversing slick jetties or negotiating the perilous rocks of Northeastern striper pursuits require much more than your choice of casual outdoor wear; but wherever you fish, the right apparel is that which minimizes hindrances and keeps you ready to fish.

Let's take a look at some of the items surf anglers may consider, from the ground up.

Whether your surf fishing involves challenging terrain and harsh conditions, or just a laidback scenario, the right apparel helps maximize your experience.

Aggressive surf casters are going to get splashed and should be prepared for it. Right, the fish still bite in the rain.

Footwear

Climate and terrain are two of the most important factors to consider in selecting footwear for surf fishing.

Climate and terrain (smooth sand, scattered shells, rocks, etc.) drive most choices for surf-fishing footwear. Folks inclined to outdoors recreation usually can handle wet feet, but unbearably cold temperatures will end your trip in a hurry. Remember, you can temporarily loosen or remove shoes that are too hot, but realizing you're ill-prepared for cold conditions requires more than a quick fix. Likewise, you don't want to go through all the effort and expense of preparing to fish that long jetty or a distant, rocky point, only to find you can't walk the unforgiving environment without risking a turned ankle or serious tumble on the slippery surface.

A variety of lightweight, water-friendly footwear for warm climates.

For beaches and piers, you can get by with most any enclosed footwear, from your leather boat shoes to those retired sneakers. Lightweight slip-ons from national brands or discount retailers offer an inexpensive option, but make sure the generally low-cut style doesn't rub the back of your ankle. (Blisters plus sand plus saltwater equals misery.)

In warm to moderate climates, zippered neoprene booties offer a good all-around choice, providing foot protection and some ankle sup-

Slip-on, zip-up, Speed Lace, Velcro—surf anglers have many footwear choices.

port for uneven terrain. On the less-demanding beach or pier surfaces, light, breathable water shoes with good arch support will keep you comfortable for long hikes to the sweet spots or just a short stroll from your truck. Water-friendly footwear like Zeko Shoes and Columbia's Powerdrain Cool PFG are made with quick-drying mesh and designed for venting/drainage so you're not sloshing all day.

Fastening styles also contribute to comfort. Laces won't kill your day, but just check them frequently, especially if you're jetty fishing, as loose laces weaken your shoe's foot support and create a tripping hazard. Zeko's design features a single Velcro strap, while the Powerdrain includes a quick, lace toggle system for tightening or loosening the shoe.

For walking jetties, beach groins and natural rocks, invest in solid footwear with ankle support and non-slip treads. Some of the more rugged bootie styles will handle light duty, but for more advanced jetty hikes or demanding excursions to unforgiving rocks like those of the Northeast, Pacific Northwest

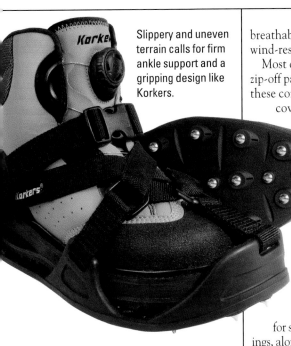

Slippery and uneven terrain calls for firm ankle support and a gripping design like Korkers.

breathable membranes offer water-resistant and wind-resistant properties.

Most outdoor apparel makers offer versatile zip-off pants in various styles. In their full form, these convertible pants provide the little bit of coverage you need to endure a chilly or buggy start to the day, while also providing a solar shield in the afternoon when you've had enough sun. In between, anglers appreciate the ability to roll up the pants to knee level for the "clam digger" look or remove the lower leg sections and convert the pants into cooler shorts. (Tip: Mark "L" and "R" on the appropriate inside seam of each zip-off leg for quick identification when it's time to restore your pants' full length.)

When choosing shorts and pants, look for styles with deep pockets and large openings, along with generous cargo pockets. The ability to carry spare tackle trays and Ziploc bags with spare bait allows you to spend more time on the front line and less time trotting back to the truck, or your beach cart. Pants and shorts with belt loops give you more options for carrying pliers, a fillet knife and other tools at your side.

or even Hawaii's lava rocks, a sturdy, lace-up wading boot with a gripping tread makes life much easier—and safer. Boots with felt soles help prevent embarrassing, if not injurious spills on slippery rocks, while Korkers—wading boots with metal gripping studs—are a must for serious rock duty.

Now, if you're the "I-don't-wear-shoes type," you probably already live in some warmer climate, but consider a few points when deciding to leave your feet unprotected. First, shell fragments, crab pincers and all types of uncomfortable little rocks have a way of finding bare feet. And if you've ever seen a catfish skeleton, you know that those serrated dorsal and pectoral spines remain just as sharp and painful long after the whiskered one expires. Complicating even minor cuts and pokes are the untold millions of microbes that could be floating through the surf, so save the fashion statement for later. Protect your feet anytime you're outdoors.

Bottoms

In all but the colder climates, swimsuits, board shorts, cut-offs and T-shirts see a lot of successful surf-fishing missions. You can wear what you prefer, but just consider that denim and other heavy fabrics hold water so once that first wave hits, you'll be wet most of the day. Shorts and fishing pants made of nylon or a nylon/cotton blend dry quickly, while those made with GORE-TEX or other waterproof,

Zip-off pants like these from Columbia quickly convert to shorts and dry quickly, too.

Tops

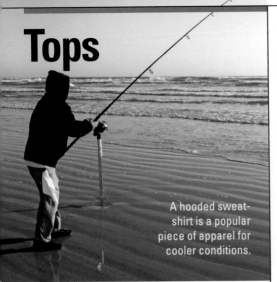

A hooded sweatshirt is a popular piece of apparel for cooler conditions.

The venerable long sleeve T-shirt espousing one's favored fishing lures, sports team, vacation city or political views will forever hold its place in the angler's wardrobe. A standalone classic or the foundation for seasonal layering, a T with sleeves that roll up for midday comfort is the essence of low-cost functionality—especially the ones with a chest pocket.

However, for not much more, you can step up to a microfiber "performance" shirt with a soft, lightweight fabric that feels like a

When choosing your surf fishing tops, you can keep it simple or go with advanced options.

feather and dries quickly. Also, the flexible fabric makes it easy to push the sleeves up above your elbow for a little air on your arms and then return them to normal length without the stretch memory that leaves a standard cotton T-shirt loose and floppy around your wrists.

Choices are many when you advance to the collared, button-up "fishing shirt," so look for the features that fit your needs. Key considerations include material (some require ironing, others remain smooth); chest pocket size, num-

ber and closures (button, hook and loop, zipper); collar design; venting style and extras like a rod holder that allows you to lean a rod against your chest and secure it with a hook and loop strap.

Other attractive features to look for in modern shirt designs include ultraviolet protection, antimicrobial treatments, insect repellant, moisture-wicking fabrics and comfort technology like Columbia's sweat-activated Omni-Freeze Zero cooling system (Columbia.com). On the aesthetic side, Columbia's Blood and Guts technology and World Wide Sportsman's NANO-tex® Resists Spills Technology (basspro.com) makes those nice shirts easy to clean when a busy day of fishing leaves them soiled.

Similar to zip-off pants, most long-sleeve fishing shirts include buttons or loops for securing rolled-up sleeves above your elbow. However, if you go with a short sleeve style and later find the heat a little too much for your arms, Columbia's Freezer Zero Arm Sleeves or Under Armour's Shooter Sleeves (underarmour.com) offer lightweight slip-on sleeves that cover your exposed arm from wrist to above the elbow.

Modern fabrics have enhanced the classic long sleeve T-shirt look with greater functionality.

Additional Protection

Experienced anglers pack a rain jacket regardless of the weather forecast. Even with no chance of precipitation, it's nice to have a little extra warmth at close reach. From a water-resistant packable windbreaker to a fleece-lined foul weather jacket, climate and personal tolerance level should guide your decision. In nastier conditions—rain or wind-driven spray—an adjustable hood with storm flap and elastic sleeve cuffs will keep the water on the outside.

For the lower body, bibs offer more coverage than waist-level rain pants, but keep in mind that the looser fit makes bibs susceptible to water intrusion unless paired with a rain jacket. The relevance there is that surf anglers occasionally employ bibs to keep wave splash off their torso when entering the surf to make a long cast.

Waders offer a better option and one that keeps you dry, feet to torso. In moderate conditions, a set of light, breathable waders like Cabela's RVG II Stockingfoot Stout will do the job. But when the water's cold, like "I'm-gonna-freeze!" cold,

Chest waders add warmth, but surf anglers find they're most helpful in repelling waves.

you'll want to be inside something made of neoprene. Sized properly, you'll have room for a light pair of pants, or better yet, a heat-holding base layer.

Generally, neoprene waders of 3- to 5-mm thickness will handle any surf fishing scenarios like the fall red drum parade along North Carolina's Outer Banks, late-season striper action off Montauk and anytime big waves pound the jetties. A 3-mm thickness may suffice, but you're usually better off with the 5-mm. Fact: You can roll down the thicker waders if they get too hot, but you can't make thin waders any warmer. For consistent

Properly dressed and protected, anglers stand the best chance of winning fights with big fish, like this hefty striped bass.

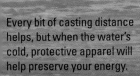

Every bit of casting distance helps, but when the water's cold, protective apparel will help preserve your energy.

Neoprene waders and dry tops help cold water anglers avoid the chill at night.

without the extra weight of water-laden waders.

Beyond wader level, Northeast striper fishermen bent on reaching the optimal casting platforms of coastal rocks often gird themselves in neoprene wetsuits. Waders and dry tops (watertight jackets) are no rarity among this crowd, but wetsuits in the 3- to 5-mm thickness allow you to cross water as deep as you care to walk or swim. Wading boots with Korkers slip over the wetsuit feet, while fleece-lined neoprene socks beneath the suit help maintain warmth and comfort.

Wetsuiters typically wear light neoprene or Lycra shorts or pants below their suits, along with a Lycra rash guard T-shirt to protect their skin against chafing. Colder conditions may warrant a tight-fitting neoprene jacket (aka "heater top") in sleeved or sleeveless form; sometimes hooded. In warmer conditions with potentially cooler nights, a wind-cutting dry top will take the edge off a midnight breeze.

stability, go with stocking-foot waders and wading boots two sizes larger than your street shoes. With boot-foot waders, getting a boot stuck in soft bottom can lead to stumbling, as your foot slips out when you try to step forward. External boots fastened against stocking foot waders lessen this risk. For added safety, cinch a wading belt around your waist to avoid swamping your waders in the event of an unexpected wave or a slip.

Stocking foot waders and external boots offer the most secure option when wading.

Also, keep a small knife in easy reach outside your waders. In the event of an unthinkable accident, cutting yourself out of compromised waders—or at least cutting drain holes—can be a life-saver. This may sound counterintuitive for cold water environments, but we're talking about a scenario in which that water has already intruded your safe zone and the top priority is getting back to safe footing—a task more easily accomplished

Keep It Clean

The smell is unmistakable—that eye-crossing stench of sea water left to dry in footwear, waders, jackets and towels. Carrying a microscopic mix of the sea's organic salad bar, briny residue delivers a rude wakeup call when you just toss that damp gear into a pile in the garage, or worse yet, leave it in the back/trunk of your vehicle.

Avoid the stench by simply rinsing your gear after each use. Whether it's the public beach shower facilities, a garden hose or the shower at home, removing the saltwater before it dries keeps your gear in tolerable condition. For a more thorough cleaning, liquid soaps are fine for shoes, towels, gear bags, etc., but remaining residues can impede the water-beading properties of synthetic materials of waders and outerwear. AquaSeal Wader Wash (www.thesurfcaster. com) and ReviveX Synthetic Fabric Cleaner (http://www.mcnett.com/gearaid/) offer cleaning options that won't compromise performance.

After cleaning, prevent mildew by thoroughly drying your gear prior to storage. Items not meant for tumble drying need only

Polarized Sunglasses

Knocking down that surface glare is important for spotting fish, bait and various bottom features. Wide frame, fit-over styles commodate prescription glasses, while some ands like Costa del Mar, Maui Jim and Ocean aves will build the lenses you want with your escription. Secure your glasses with a neck rap—preferably one with a built-in float. For a omemade option, slide a cigar float onto a piece 40-pound fluorocarbon, drill a small hole at e tip of each arm, thread one tip of your fluoro hrough each hole and secure with crimps.

A quality pair of polarized glasses will block harmful glare, improve your ability to see into the water and minimize eye fatigue.

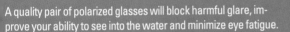

insing your apparel after each use extends its life.

couple of hours in the sunshine. Gear hung side takes longer to dry, but with decent air rculation, you'll be fine. Wherever you dry our gear, hang it for maximum surface expoure—no piling over the fence post—and hang ems as straight as possible so they retain their riginal shape, without seam-wearing creases.

Standard garment hangers work for outwear, but waders present a challenge, as ou'll want to angle them downward to allow all noisture to drain from the feet/leg sections. The l-steel Rack 'Em Snake Waders Hanger (Caelas.com) offers a convenient option that holds vaders upside-down by the feet. Probably the est option for drying waders, boots and shoes is thermal dryer (Peetshoedryer.com).

Gaiters will keep sand, shells and beach grit ut of wading boots, but it's nearly npossible to keep these annoynces out of lower cut shoes. A imple dunk in the waves generlly clears out the intruding matter, ut it's no rarity to carry part of

the beach home with you, so give your footwear a good rinsing outside your house. Two big thoughts here—first, washing sand and grit down your sink or shower drains can create clogging issues. Also, tossing dirty beach shoes into the drier typically leaves a mound of sand and shell fragments at the bottom of the bin and—speaking from experience—I can assure you that such things do not go over well with the lady of the house.

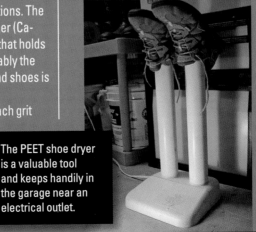

The PEET shoe dryer is a valuable tool and keeps handily in the garage near an electrical outlet.

Headwear

Shielding your head from the sun helps reduce fatigue, not to mention the chances of skin cancer.

Long-bill caps or any wide-brim hat used in conjunction with polarized glasses will block sun glare and improve overall beach vision. Some fishing shirt designs include fold-out collars that fasten to the back of your hat for neck protection. Hats like the World Wide Sportsman XPS Boda Boonie Hat or Columbia's Bug Me Not Cachalot include built-in neck shades and, of course, a bandana or T-shirt under your hat will accomplish the same.

If windy conditions threaten to displace a hat or cap, consider a beanie-style cap for head warmth. Buffs, hoods and lightweight neck gaiters provide wind and sun protection, while pulling the flexible fabric over the back of your cap holds it steady in the wind.

A lightweight neck gaiter, worn by author David A. Brown, offers a versatile sun-protection accessory. During intense sunlight, the gaiter can be moved to shield most of the face, neck and head.

This pier angler uses a hat with neck shield and a kerchief to keep the sun at bay.

Thick neoprene gloves, such as the Pro Series Angler Gloves from Buff (above) provide durable construction to protect hands from low temperatures and rough surfaces. Tailin' Toads (below) provides lightweight sun gloves to protect skin from solar damages.

Gloves

Even in tolerable temperatures, neoprene gloves like the Aquaskinz Black Thunder (Aquaskinz.com) protect your hands from barnacle-covered rocks, prevent cuts and scrapes while shucking shellfish for fresh bait, and eliminate those nasty line cuts when leadering big fish. Fingerless models like Cabela's WindShear Fishing Gloves offer wind and cold protection with optimal dexterity, while various lightweight "sun gloves" shield hands from harmful UV rays.

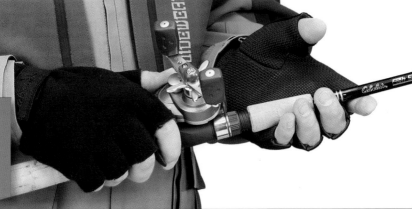

Fingerless handwear like Cabela's WindShear Gloves offer protection and dexterity.

Sunscreen & Sun Protection

A hot bite can make you miss lunch, ignore your cell phone and skip the bathroom break, but don't start your day without lathering on sunscreen with a Sun Protection Factor (SPF) of at least 30. Be sure to wash your hands with the old surf-and-sand rinse after applying sunscreen creams to avoid transferring the scent to your baits.

With spray, cream and stick forms, sunscreens are fast and easy to apply to kids.

Hat, sunglasses, neck gaiter—you can never have too much sun protection. Below, shade from the Sunbrella.

First Aid

Carry a well-stocked first aid kit to handle fishing's occasional incidents and accidents. AdventureMedicalKits.com offers a range of kit sizes, including a marine lineup of waterproof boxes stocked with bandages, wound care items, forceps and other essentials. Basic packages will handle minor cuts, pokes and bites, but the more distant your fishing spots and the more rigorous your level of activity, the more you should consider a more advanced kit that contains a deeper stock of wound care and dressing items, along with the supplies and instruments to address sprains/fractures, serious bleeding, CPR needs and emergency field treatments. A pair of diagonal cutters sturdy enough to cut a hook will come in handy one day.

When those unforeseen accidents occur, you'll appreciate a well-stocked first aid kit.

In areas of possible jellyfish and Portuguese man-o-war encounters, add a shaker bottle of meat tenderizer to your first aid kit, as the ingredients that soften steaks also neutralize the venom transferred during a sting. Other beachside treatments include vinegar, Isopropyl ("rubbing") alcohol and lemon or lime juice. (For serious or allergic reactions to any sting, seek medical attention.) To reduce the pain of a stingray or saltwater catfish spine wound, apply hot water immediately and continually, as hot as you can tolerate without harming yourself. Seek medical attention quickly to prevent infection.

Note to self: Reeling fishing line through a jellyfish or man-o-war can leave fresh tentacles on your line and all those little stinging cells remain active long enough for a parting shot. Take it from a past victim: Dangling tentacles are fully capable of delivering a painful sting, so use a towel, or a handful of beach sand to safely rub the intruder from your line.

Even when we're cautious, fishing presents various risks. Fortunately, most related injuries can be treated well on the spot.

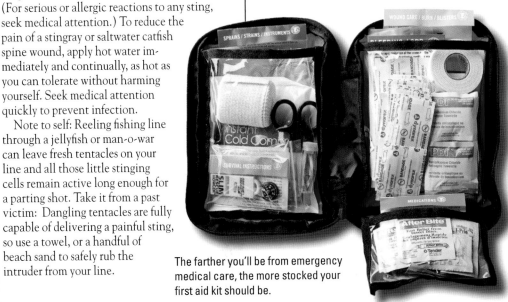

The farther you'll be from emergency medical care, the more stocked your first aid kit should be.

CHAPTER 5

Techniques & Tools of the Trad

Where-to and how-to details vary greatly throughout the 12,380 miles of U.S. coastline, but we'll look at representative regional samplings starting in Chapter 9. In any region, the skills of finding fish stand essential to catching them with any degree of regularity. Such skills also vary from state to state, but a handful of general principles provide the basis for good surf fishing acumen. Consider the basic notions here and you'll quickly fine tune them to your own waters.

Wherever you fish and whatever your targets, understanding what goes on in and around the surf will improve your productivity.

Big stripers like this
one won't make
it easy on you, so
pay attention to the
conditions and adjust
as needed.

Keep it Comfortable

Long days on the beach are more tolerable when you know you've packed the necessary comfort items.

Nurses, waitresses, car salesmen—they all know what surf anglers eventually discover—spending a lot of time on your feet causes fatigue and that can limit effective performance. As noted in Chapter 4, proper footwear provides an important foundation, but one of the most common points of fatigue is lower back pain. Age and physical condition factor here, but a few simple points will improve your comfort and keep you in good shape for the surf action.

Back Up Your Back

Lumbar support belts won't cure pre-existing lower back issues, but they provide support that keeps you properly aligned and helps prevent strains and pains from the awkward turns and twists that happen when waves push you off balance, or that slick jetty rock sends you sliding. Cabela's makes a Back Support Wading Belt that doubles as a safety belt to prevent waders from filling up with water, while Simms Back Magic Wading Belt features an orthopedic design for cases of more severe back discomfort. Elsewhere, pharmacies and home supply stores offer standard lumbar support belts.

Planning for your comfort, safety and mobility is just as important as packing the right surf-fishing tackle.

Lumbar support belts will minimize fatigue and keep you in the game longer.

Take a Seat

A few minutes off your feet gives your spinal column and back muscles a much needed break. Folding camp chairs come in a wide variety of styles and sizes from simple stools to cozy loungers with sun shades. If you like to pick a spot and stay there for a couple of hours at a time, indulge in something nap-worthy and take a break when you find yourself doing the old lumbar lean. Conversely, if yours is the run-and-gun style, a compact Ascend Tech Folding Trail Chair (Basspro.com) sits right on the sand with a strap-supported 90-degree back rest and folds into a double cushion with carrying handles.

Bring water to the beach—in plastic bottles, or even better, in large, reusable containers to keep waste minimal.

Beach chairs make the slower periods more comfortable.

Stay Hydrated

The body needs water for all critical functions and running low can lead to muscular cramps, fatigue and overall weakness. A good rule of thumb for quantity is to take half your body weight in pounds and drink that number of ounces daily. (A 180-pound person should drink 90 ounces of water daily.) Sports beverages with electrolytes are also helpful, but Livestrong.com suggests making your own sports beverage by bolstering distilled water with a pinch of sea salt for electrolytes, citrus juice (calcium and potassium) and honey (glucose).

Keep It Loose

Stretching exercises will help prepare your body for the exertion and physical demands of strenuous surf fishing activities. Troy Lindner, a freshwater tournament pro and licensed health and fitness practitioner, offers angler-friendly exercise and fitness videos at Fit4Fishing.com. Build a few minutes of stretching into your fishing routine and if your day finds fatigue setting in, take a break for these on-the-spot exercises.

A few minutes of stretching will minimize potential injuries.

Find Your Spot

When Jacksonville surf pro David Gill selects a spot along one of Florida's East Coast beaches, he makes observation his first priority. He calls it "listening to the water." The surf, he said, will tell you what's going on and those who pay attention will quickly dial in the promising areas.

Gill starts by surveying the breakers and looks for higher spots that indicate a more prominent bar section below. Bar tops are where the most dramatic forage upheavals occur and that's where pompano, permit and sharks typically hunt. Even at the end of a wave, where the water spreads across the sand like a smooth sheet, there's enough energy remaining to uncover and scatter tiny clams the size of M&Ms. Look closely as a wave recedes and once the froth clears, you'll see dozens of those little shellfish pop themselves into a vertical stance and wriggle into total sandy concealment.

Note the boundaries of shallow (lighter) water and deeper (dark) water.

"Listen" to the water and it will lead you to the areas of highest surf-fishing potential.

This happens, in greater degree, every time a wave hits a sandbar—the water's full force uncovers thousands of clams, sand fleas or whatever local forage exists and sends these morsels billowing into the turbulence. Some make it back to the safety of the sand; many do not, but

A back-current formed by the collision of an incoming wave with a lingering outgoing wave stirs up the beach and dislodges forage like sand fleas (inset).

Egrets hunting minnows around a jetty during low tide offer a good indication of the structure's high-water potential.

Jetties harbor various forage such as crabs, which attract predators.

Runouts help anglers identify key fishing spots where the surf concentrates forage. ▶

understanding the timing of this activity helps anglers properly place their baits for the fish that feed atop the bars and then anticipate the bites.

On the beach, Texas surf guide Marcus Heflin looks for signs of crossing water—waves receding in angled sections that often join to form a foamy V. Such evidence of multiple currents indicates an area of higher energy and that means more bottom disturbance to attract predators. Equally promising are tightly formed run-outs, which point to sub-surface drains that may extend a football field-plus into the surf. Just like a marsh feeder creek, these food lanes are game fish magnets.

Surf anglers seeking active areas also watch for back-currents, clearly defined by a nearly vertical wall of "brown water" created when the remainder of one wave lingers long enough to collide with the next one's arrival. The opposing forces create a momentary stalemate in which the calmer outgoing water stands up against the frothing new wave, with the result looking something like an angel food cake with whipped vanilla frosting.

Alabama surf angler Mike Kennedy notes that tidal dynamics will occasionally carve out semicircular depressions, or "bowls" in the bottom. Any such change in depth and contour presents a focal point for predators, which take advantage of concentrated forage accumulation and the ability

The dynamics of surf fishing may appear subtle, but their influences are most profound.

to ambush passing prey by holding in these bowls during lighter surf conditions.

Other promising beach signs include clusters of freshly cracked mollusk shells and pieces of crab—indications of nearby feeding. Direct evidence of local forage includes ghost shrimp mounds (holes in muddy banks), tiny sand balls next to a recently-excavated fiddler crab burrow and the V-shaped wakes of receding waves breaking over dislodged sand fleas digging into the beach. Sharks teeth require strong currents to make the trip from offshore ranges, so finding a few on your beach stands as a promising sign.

While crustacean, mollusk and invertebrate forage species usually hold their ground, run-outs, cross currents and other surf dynamics will change throughout the day. Some anglers will pick a promising area, set up shop and take what the sea delivers, while others keep moving to stay on top of the key beach features and the fish they attract. Now, despite these commonly occurring points of piscatorial probability, you may occasionally find fish on seemingly featureless areas of the beach. Could be coincidence, or the fish might have been moving from one preferable area to the next and stumbled across your bait. Sharks, big jacks and other predators will often scatter local groupings, while excessive fishing pressure has a predictably disruptive effect—especially when weekends and holidays see a higher propensity for overcrowding key spots.

When schools of glass minnow or other baitfish gather in the shallow surf, predators like snook and tarpon often move in close to feed.

If you don't like sitting in one spot all day, pack light and stay mobile.

Eyes on the Prize

No doubt, surf fishing requires a lot of blind casting, but observant types are wise to spend the down time between bites closely watching the surf for signs of fish. Breaking water, sudden splashes, boils, leaping baitfish—all signal something happening beneath the surface. In a rolling surf off Florida's Melbourne Beach, you may catch just a glimpse, maybe the shadow or flash of a fish moving through the waves, while a calm day off Gulf Shores, Alabama, may allow you to spot flounder on the bottom or speckled trout chasing bait at the end of a long cast.

Sunlight greatly benefits the surf angler's recon, while clouds dim the scene and cast confusing shadows over the water. The low angles of early morning and late afternoon light make for softer, eye-friendly illumination, but midday sun brings harsh glare that actually challenges your vision. Polarized sunglasses are essential for seeing through the glimmer and a hat with a dark brim reduces the glare that can bounce from the water and into your face. (If your hat has lighter fabric under the brim, darken it with a black, brown or navy blue permanent marker.)

Anglers on jetties and piers benefit from elevated views, but beach anglers are well served to scout

Surf anglers must learn to work with prevailing sky conditions when searching for fish.

the surf zone from high ground. Making friends with pier bait shop staff or regular pier anglers can help garner valuable insight on conditions and bait schools, as well as that all-important heads-up on approaching game fish with just a phone call or text. Another option for surf recon: Use a 5-gallon bucket for a beachside observation tower. If the surf is calm enough to use this tool off the beach, use a bucket with a lid so your weight doesn't push the narrow rim into the sand. A two-step kitchen utility ladder offers a little more height with greater stability, but narrow legs sink quickly, so fit them with broader foot pads made from tennis balls.

Polarized sunglasses are essential for spotting bait schools and the predator fish that they attract.

When low light, turbid water or high surf limits your visibility, look to the sky for assistance. A cluster of birds hovering near the surface or circling a tight area means predators like striped bass, bluefish, mackerel or false albacore are chasing baitfish just below the surface. Gulls, terns and other seabirds pick off the scraps each time the fish pin their prey at the surface so monitor these aerial indicators for cues on approaching action.

Similarly, New England surf casters often coexist with boat anglers who close in on the same striped bass schools that run the nearshore rocks. Ideally, everyone cooperates for mutual benefit, but an approaching flotilla certainly indicates good things ahead for the guys in waders and wetsuits. For both user groups, strong winds reposition local forage (bunker, aka menhaden) and stripers will follow.

On the other hand, surf anglers interested in wading and sight fishing prefer calmer areas with optimal visibility. In the northern Gulf of Mexico, two major estuaries—Alabama's Mobile Bay and Louisiana's Mississippi River Delta—pump voluminous flows of muddy water into the coastal areas. Throughout this region, tides and wind direction push the murky water, so those who enjoy looking for their targets pay close attention to how daily conditions affect clarity.

Walking Staff

Negotiating jetties, rocky outcroppings and any uneven surface can prove tricky, if not hazardous, especially when a pounding surf challenges your every step. When moving out to make a long cast, a walking staff provides an extra point of contact to help maintain your balance and footing. The collapsible FolStaff (Cabelas.com), with its cork handle and carbide tip, springs into a locked position for walking support and then breaks down to a 9-inch package that fits in a belt holster.

Inexpensive homemade models can be fashioned from PVC, a broom handle or a wooden dowel (1-inch diameter). Wrap the end you'll hold with electrical or athletic tape for better gripping (and splinter avoidance), drill a hole one inch from the top, thread it with the cord of your choice and tie the cord to form a strap wide enough to sling across your neck and arm while casting. For quick stowage, wedging the staff into a rock crevice keeps it in place while you attend to a fish or rigging need.

Jetties offer surf anglers access to deeper water with an emergent reef system, but traversing the uneven surfaces requires a cautious step.

St. Croix's 2-piece Avid rod has a wading staff tip in the butt section.

Perpendicular casts may be most common, but don't hesitate to cast at an angle if you see the chance for a hookup.

Fish could be just about anywhere throughout the surf zone, so cast where you can and then focus on where strikes occur.

All in the Angles

Given the water dynamics and elongated structure, fish could be just about anywhere along a pier or jetty, so casts in any unobstructed angle make perfect sense. On the beach, perpendicular casts are certainly most common, but at times, other options are prudent. The most common adjustment is a 45-degree angle cast that helps establish proper bait positioning in a strong current. Say you're trying to line up your bait with a runout or hit the high spot on a sand bar but the swiftness of the longshore current pulls your bait away from the target zone before your Sputnik sinker can dig into the sand. No worries, just cast upcurrent and let the water sweep your bait down to your intended spot. It may take a couple of shots to dial in the appropriate lead distance, but once you figure it out, the formula should hold steady (with gradual adjustments for tide stage).

In a couple of scenarios, you may also want to fish parallel to the shore. Notwithstanding targets

When an active surf makes it tough for even a Sputnik style sinker to set, cast upcurrent and give your weight time to dig in before reaching your target zone.

of opportunity (i.e. predators chasing a bait school into the shallows), fish often feed right along the shoreline in what's called "the drop"—a distinct little ledge that sometimes forms along higher impact beaches as waves gnaw away at the sandy slope. Predators will use this lane similar to a trough between bars, so work the area with jigs or drag light Carolina rigs with indigenous baits.

When summer finds snook spawning near Gulf of Mexico passes, the fish will spend all but the full and new moon periods feeding along adjacent beaches, often so shallow that their pale yellow fins break the water. At times, casting more than a dozen feet off the sand means you're fishing behind the snook. They're not always that tight, but linesiders tend to establish a depth they prefer and most of the fish will stay pretty close to that corridor. Wading the warm beach brine and working baits through this zone usually keeps you in the fish.

Whether you're plug casting, sight fishing with synthetic shrimp or chunking natural baits, several tools will aid your surf fishing efforts.

Pliers

Helpful for all those little gripping, turning and tuning jobs, beach-friendly pliers should be corrosion resistant with sturdy side cutters that'll trim braided line or wire. Needle nose pliers (or forceps) help you reach hooks in toothy mouths or extract those deeply set.

If you wear belted pants or shorts, pliers with a looped holster are most secure, with clip-on sheaths a good option with or without a belt. When heavy jackets and bibs make it tough to quickly reach pliers affixed to your waist, just stick them in a closeable outer pocket. In this scenario, pliers without lanyards linking them to sheaths afford easier handling; unless the sheath can clip to the seam of your jacket pocket.

Lip Grippers & Catch Device

From Boga Grips to durable plastic grippers (thefishgrip.net), you'll appreciate a device that's safe for you and the fish when hauling a hefty one out of the surf or lifting a toothy catch for photos.

A tail rope or Fish Tailer (AFTCO.com) allows you to secure a shark or other large fish by the tail to haul it ashore for dehooking.

Lip grippers, like this one by Rapala, make it easy and safe to handle fish or one with lots of teeth.

Wading belts with lanyards and slots for pliers and other tools come handy when you walk the surf.

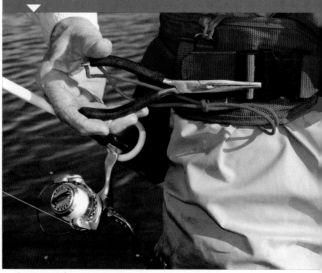

Think of all the different tasks and operations you may need to undertake and equip yourself with the right tools.

Pier & Jetty Tools

Considering the often long—sometimes arduous—journey to your fishing spot, you won't have the luxury of dashing back to the vehicle each time you need something, so map out your fishing plan ahead of time and make a check list of each item you might need. Pier cart space or your personal load tolerance will dictate how much you can carry, but limit yourself to the truly necessary—especially on space-limited jetties.

Some piers have bait prep stations and benches, but planning for self-reliance (the only option for jetties) avoids space conflicts. A piece of wood with a low frame makes a handy cutting board, while keeping sinkers and baits from slipping off the edge. (Make it yourself from scrap lumber or salvage from junk items like a discarded chest.)

On fishing piers, buckets serve as (short-term) bait tanks, wash-up sinks and places to hold your catch (lacking a cooler). Filling a bucket from a pier's elevation can be tricky, as they're often difficult to turn over—especially in windy conditions. Eliminate this frustration by either attaching lead weight to one side of the bucket's rim (ideally at a point aligned with the handle's center), or affixing a weight to the base of your rope clip, which connects to the handle. When you drop the bucket, the weight pulls the rim downward for easy fill-ups. Cloth rope of about ¼-inch diameter has a hand-friendly surface, but gloves with a gripping surface will minimize the calluses.

For landing big fish from piers, long-handle gaffs on wooden poles, rope gaffs (large, weighted treble hook on a rope), or rope-mounted hoop nets (Frabill.com) are the common tools. On jetties, a telescoping landing net (Cummings.com) proves helpful when water level and rock angles make for challenging reaches. For long-distance scooping, modify a long-handle pool cleaning net with a larger frame and mesh that'll stand up to the saltwater environment.

Adding lead weight to your 5-gallon bucket's clip-rope tips the rim forward and enables you to fill the bucket from a pier.

Piers and jetties usually require long walks, so think about all you'll need and try to carry everything in one trip.

Carts facilitate gear transport on piers and paved jetties.

Casting Call

Reels lacking line guides require manual guidance for even spool coverage.

Complementing appropriate tackle selection with effective casting techniques will ensure effective bait/lure presentations. Individual styles generally develop with personal experience, but a handful of basic styles will equip you for most any surf fishing scenario and provide a foundation for situational modifications.

You'll need to employ good casting form for optimal presentations.

Pendulum Cast

Used in various forms by distance casting competitors, the pendulum technique can lengthen your casts when you need to reach those outer spots (especially helpful on low tide). Start with your back at a 45 degree angle to the water with a high rod posture pointing toward the beach. Push the rod back to swing the bait away from you and as it starts to return forward, redirect the momentum to the side opposite your casting lane. This secondary step establishes the energy for your cast, so as that pendulum angle loads the rod, rotate your body toward the water as you guide the rod around to release the cast at the appropriate angle.

Open Beach Cast

Given its intuitive nature, the overhead is probably the most commonly used option among surf anglers, but precise technique influences effectiveness. Face the water at a 45-degree angle and grip the rod with one hand at the reel and the other at the very base of the rod butt. With the rod extending over

Overhead Power Cast

Given its intuitive nature, the overhead is probably the most commonly used option among surf anglers, but precise technique influences effectiveness. Face the water at

A simple, intuitive technique makes the Overhead Power Cast a good choice for many scenarios.

your back shoulder, check your clearance, swing the rod back to load up, and as you pull forward with your top arm, push down on the butt with your other arm. Often overlooked, that downward lever motion significantly increases your overall power and expands your casts.

Effective casting form increases your surf catches.

You'll gain casting distance by standing in the surf, but watch wave action for safety's sake.

your target spot and grip the rod with one hand at the reel and the other at the very base of the rod butt. With the rod extending over your back shoulder, check your clearance, let the sinker onto the sand and as you pull forward with your top arm, push

down on the butt with your other arm. Often overlooked, that downward lever motion significantly increases your overall power and extends your casts.

As the rod loads, use your forward hand to push the rod butt downward for maximum casting force.

Complete the cast with a fluid and powerful overhead motion and release the line at the proper angle.

Pier Casting

Always check that the space behind you is clear before making a big cast from a pier.

Limited space and an often-cluttered environment make long casting difficult, but not impossible. On an uncrowded T pier (or one with cooperative fellow anglers), lay your rig on open pavement behind you for maximum extension and cast when ready. For longer casts from a pier's main span, stand close to the guard rail opposite your casting side, extend your rod as far as possible with the tip at a 45-degree angle and with one fluid movement, launch your cast as you trot toward the other guardrail. Timing is key and you want to make sure your rig is heading upward before your rod's forward motion raises it level with the handrail or you can expect a very short cast. (The same principle works on jetties, but consider that your rig will hang close to the rocks, so make sure nothing snags before whipping the rod forward.)

On crowded days where back swings are not possible, use the space under the pier to your advantage. Start by holding the rod straight down with about four to six feet of line between the tip and your rig. Swing the rig back under the pier to load up and then snap the rod forward to release the cast at 10 o'clock.

For more on surf casting techniques, check out Nickaway Media's instructional DVD series featuring the "Stop-Point" teaching method and a casting aid (rope segment with handles) that helps casters learn proper hand positioning (www.nickaway.com/). Also, surf casting pro Ron Arra offers one-on-one instruction, along with his book "The Ultimate Guide to Surf Casting." (http://www.ronarrasurfpro.com/).

On crowded days where back swings are not possible, use the space under the pier to cast.

Nabbing sur-
face-feeding
mackerel of-
ten requires
a quick,
pinpoint cast.

Timing your pier casts also
includes keeping clear of
incoming waves in rough surf.

Usually there's plenty of room
on piers for all who want to
fish, as long as cooperation is
the prevailing spirit.

CHAPTER 6

Gear for Catching & Keeping

Notwithstanding the simple and spontaneous option of one rod and a small tackle bag, serious surf fishing operations can include a considerable amount of gear and transporting everything to the seashore requires logistical planning. Most surf rods break down to fit inside your vehicle, but the sport's devotees mount vertical rod holders to their bumpers or install angled holders in pickup truck beds (RodRack.com). Industrious types may opt for building a wooden frame to horizontally hang or notch their rods in their truck bed. Similarly, heavy duty aluminum cooler racks with built-in rod holders keep your gear centralized on the front or rear bumper (beachfishingcarts.com).

Florida surf angler David Gill has tricked out his Jeep with bumper-mounted gear carts that allow him to drive his entire operation up and down beaches like New Smyrna.

There's nothing wrong with walking to the beach with a single rod and a small bag of tackle, but the more involved your surf fishing becomes, the more gear you'll probably need.

Properly tooled anglers can expect to pull impressive catches from the surf.

Go the Distance

In many locales, ferries transport trucks to barrier islands for remote fishing, but bring all you need.

When traveling to distant shores, a durable plastic rod case or a homemade container fashioned from PVC with threaded caps strapped to your luggage rack saves interior space for passengers. The Titan Rod Vault (Cabelas.com) holds rods up to 10 feet (or longer rods broken down) in an aerodynamic aluminum case with a locking clamp that attaches to most roof racks.

For beaches that do not allow vehicle access, hiking with a load of gear can be an exhausting chore for anyone, regardless of physical ability. Backpacks or waterproof duffle bags will accommodate the gear for minimalists committed to artificials and packaged natural baits, but if you're transporting live baits, coolers and more than a couple of rods, you'll want some type of cart.

Standard aluminum frame carts with pull handles and a few rod holders are available at most coastal tackle shops, or online (beachfishingcarts.com).

After a few trips, surf anglers may opt to customize their carts to suit their personal style and gear needs with additional rod holders, bait tray/cutting board, side storage, and wider beach tires for traversing loose sand or soft beach sand more easily.

I once saw a guy pedaling a bike with a modified wagon jerryrigged to the rear fender. This enabled him to tow a tackle box, rods and assorted gear across a paved jetty. Creative types with more ingenuity than endurance could easily modify a 3-wheeled "trike" to accommodate enough gear for a day on the beach. For light beach duty (i.e. short walks), piers or paved jetties, grocery style pull carts (ex. from Home Depot, etc.) will suffice, although modifications like larger wheels, PVC rod holders and a water resistant liner will improve functionality.

Light packers may consider a "gear sled" fashioned from a plastic model (Sledwarehouse.com). Made for zipping over ice and snow, these

> **I once saw a guy pedaling a bike with a modified wagon jerry-rigged to the rear fender.**

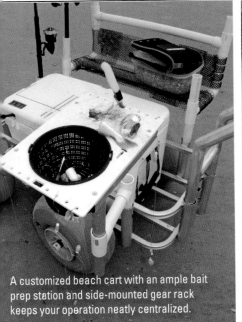

A customized beach cart with an ample bait prep station and side-mounted gear rack keeps your operation neatly centralized.

A standard beach cart will serve the basic purpose, but custom add-ons include wider wheels (below left) and a pop-up umbrella (below right).

sleds make short work of beach sand—either dry and loose or damp and compacted. Walk in a few inches of calm water and the floating sled moves with ease. Alabama guide David Thornton customized a 48-incher by adding a wooden frame with PVC rod holders and space for a tackle bag and cooler. Boogie boards—even the inexpensive ones sold at every surf shop—are easily modified with basic elements such as a milk crate (sold at office supply stores), PVC rod holders and ratchet straps to hold the main tackle container in place.

Gear sleds built on floating bases can also double as wading caddies, although products like the Ultimate Wade Fishing Caddy (ultimatewade-fishingcaddy.com) provide a task-specific option. Texas surf wading guide Marcus Heflin modified a commercially made caddy, but his enhancements can also inspire anglers who start from scratch with a large block of foam. Heflin beefed up the interior elements with heavier binding materials and added weights around the edges for stability. He also added an extra rod holder with bungee cords to secure rods in each holder, a small plastic box for tackle and a holster for his needle nose pliers and knife.

Wading caddies excel in deeper water where you may find yourself chest deep at times. For shallower scenarios, a wading belt (wadeaid.com) simplifies the operation by putting key gear items such as pliers, knife, stringer and hand towel on your waist.

Beach carts provide invaluable service when access to the surf requires a long hike through soft sand.

This beach cart made from a snow sled skids along the sand with minimal resistance.

A rod butt stuck in sand offers little resistance to a strike. You're better off grabbing a PVC or aluminum rod holder before walking the beach.

reports from elsewhere along the beach, investing in protective products such as LifeProof, Otterbox Armor Series and Aquapac Cell Phone Case allows you to use your phone with no worry of water damage. If you're uncomfortable leaving a wallet unattended in your gear bag while wading or walking out for long casts, a Cabela's Surf Safe Container keeps a driver's license, credit cards, cash and a maybe a single car key in a lightweight sealable, watertight box with a neck cord. You can also loop the cord around a belt and tuck the container securely in your pocket.

From beach carts and wading caddies, to dry bags and cell phone cases, surf anglers have many options for how they carry their gear and valuables.

If you're wearing waders, the gap between the cinch of your wading belt and the top edge of the waders makes a convenient spot for a small tackle tray. For a more secure option, keep spare tackle and lures in a small chest pack or a sling style tackle bag that fits around like a guitar strap for easy rotation from an idle position on your back, to front and center. Regardless of how much time you actually spend standing in the water, you'll want to plan for the protection of your valuables. No matter how waterproof you consider your tackle bag, moisture has a way of breaching the most secure containers—if by no other means than wet hands reaching inside. A small dry bag tucked in there with the tackle trays will protect your wallet, keys, etc. (In a pinch, a Ziploc bag gets the job done.)

Because it's good to keep cell phones handy for catch photos and scouting

This surf angler is all smiles after the gear she carried to the beach helped produce this nice pompano.

Taking a Stand

Far Left: This angler went with an aluminum sand spike that features foot pegs for better setting leverage.

Left: Sea Striker Surf Pal Sand Spikes have a cutting board and mini bait stations.

Natural bait fishermen typically set multiple rods to maximize their coverage of the area and present different baits and rigs to see what the fish prefer. Obviously, holding more than one at a time isn't operationally feasible, while laying them on a beach risks sand in your reels and leaning rods against a cooler is a great way to donate your outfit to the sea, courtesy of a big redfish, shark or ray. That's why sand spikes (rod holders for the beach) are the necessary nannies of surf rods—it's all about keeping them safe and properly positioned.

Commercially made sand spikes of aluminum, PVC or a combination are available at coastal tackle shops and online retailers, while most regions with a vibrant surf fishing community find a local specialist making custom spikes for those who like their gear a certain way. Some of the details are preferential, while some are truly practical. One of the key elements of a more advanced design is a foot piece that allows you to apply more pressure when sinking the spike.

Other important features include a bolt or stopping device to limit how deeply a long rod butt fits into the holder. Rod tension will keep it secure with less than a foot of butt section in the holder, but if you insert the rod all the way to the reel seat, you'll have a tough time pulling it out of the holder when it's tightened with the pressure of a big fish.

For a simple do-it-yourself sand spike, Georgia angler Spud Woodward offers this plan: Take an 8-foot piece of 1 ½-inch diameter schedule 20 PVC and cut it in half with a 45-degree angle. This yields two 4-foot pieces, each with a flat top and an angled bottom. For a rod stopper, drill a hole about 8 inches down from the top edge and insert a stainless steel eye bolt. This not only controls the rod depth, but it also provides a handy attachment point for clipping a bait bucket or fish stringer.

Whatever design you chose, be sure to set your sand spike securely—and depth isn't the only consideration. Wiggling the spike back and forth to work it into the beach will loosen adjacent sand so always wiggle it side to side, parallel to the surf line. Wiggling a sand spike forward and backward—toward the surf and away from it—loosens sand facing the water and that can lead to a washout where waves erode the weakened area around your spike and compromise its stability.

Rod rack frames secured to a pickup truck bed offer an option for transporting gear.

You'll want cutting shears to trim baits like this blue crab.

Knives

A sturdy fillet knife can pull double duty for cleaning your catch and prepping baits, but a small bait knife offers convenience and safety with a more manageable tool that easily stores in a tackle tray or the cup holder of a surf cart. (Folding pocket knives also fit this need.) If you're using fresh oysters, clams or any bivalve mollusk for bait, add a shucking knife to your tackle bag.

With any non-folding knife, belt loop or waistband clips keep these cutting instruments at a safe distance, but resist the temptation of holding even a small open blade in your pocket. The uneven footing common to surf fishing can compromise balance and lead to anything from a slight stutter step to a full-on stumble, so never leave a blade unguarded. The same goes for bare hooks, jig heads and lures—always have a barrier between you and the point or edge.

Hook Removers

Note: In the Gulf of Mexico, anglers fishing natural baits for any reef fish species (groupers, snappers, triggerfish, etc.) are required to keep a hook remover handy. Since some of these fish are occasionally taken from piers and jetties, don't get caught without this tool. (Non-stainless steel circle hooks are also required for Gulf reef fish.)

Weights & Measures

You might get away with bluffing your buddies with less-than-accurate dimensional reports on the fish you catch, but unlike bragging rights, fisheries regulations demand precision. The eyeball method (a.k.a. the "Looks about right" method) won't cut it when the local fisheries officers decide to visit the beach or check coolers in the parking lot. Handheld digital scales help keep you honest with the forum posts, while a Florida Sportsman Law Stick keeps you right with the regs. (A cloth measuring tape, sold at craft/fabric stores, offers a convenient and water-friendly option.)

For sharks or any large fish that won't lay still for measuring, fasten a snap clip to the top end of your measuring tape (there's usually a metal grommet here for hanging). With your catch at hand, clip the tape to your leader, let the top end slide down to the fish's nose and then stretch out the tape to the fish's tail. Depending on your rig, the top end may not end up level with the fish's nose, so just note the overage and subtract this from your overall length for an accurate measurement.

Shears

Big redfish, drum and other crustacean eaters will grab a whole crab, but trimming and sectioning these baits has its benefits. First, cutting any fresh bait stimulates fish by releasing more scent and revealing the colorful innards. From a practical standpoint, a live crab—even one with a hook in its shell—isn't going to stand still and be eaten, whereas a freshly cut crustacean with even greater scent appeal won't run from predators. Lastly, fish that aren't big enough to consume an entire adult blue crab would readily gobble a knuckle (base of an arm). Shears also provide a more controlled option for cutting strips of clam, squid, etc.

Food Storage

If you plan on consuming your catch in under a

Filleting and vacuum-sealing your fish on the beach enables you to better manage your cooler space.

week, you can get away with a simple Ziploc bag in the fridge. If it's going to be longer, sealing your fillets in air-tight bags will prep them for the freezer. (Vacuum sealing is never a bad idea, even for a few days in the fridge.)

Counter-top models are fine for kitchen use,

but ZipVac makes a rechargeable handheld device for outdoors use (zip-vac.com). When connected to the vent port on one of its matching storage bags, the unit quickly vacuums out the air and leaves you with a sealed container that you can toss in the cooler until you're home.

DinnerTime

When local regulations allow beachside cooking, frying or pan searing your fresh catch over a propane camp stove makes a great complement to the surf fishing experience. Wind guards help keep sand off your meal, while double-burner models allow you to prep a side dish like baked beans along with the main course. (Coleman.com)

Coolers

Size and style generally come down to your needs for quantity, durability and functionality. Styrofoam jobs will keep the beverages cold when you're just mixing a little surf fishing with beach bopping on a family vacation, but ongoing interest merits something with greater longevity.

Soft-sided coolers pack easier and are usually less expensive than a quality rigid cooler, but the latter also offers a place to sit, a work bench for rigging and bait cutting and a handy measuring table if you take time to mark off the inches (with relevant species limits noted accordingly). Rigid coolers are less likely to leak and they typically maintain interior temperature longer than Styrofoam or soft sides.

In the absence of a cooler, you can keep your fresh catch fresh by digging a pit about a foot deep in the moist beach sand, depositing your fish and then loosely covering it with the excavated mud. Holding your fish at the cooler depth maintains freshness for about an hour or so, depending on climate. Bleeding and gutting fish is a standard practice for some, but don't cut your fish in any way, as this hastens the ill effects of bacteria. Also, be sure to mark your earthen cooler, as moist beach sand has a way of settling and hiding any evidence of digging.

Around jetties and porous rock shorelines such as Hawaii's lava rocks, isolated tide pools can serve as temporary holding tanks for keepers and even a few smaller

fish with forthcoming live-bait roles. A few things to keep in mind here: First, monitor the tide stage. Once the water rises and overtakes a tide pool, the door's open for your catch to swim or drift away. Also, unless you're on private property, you can't control who strolls past your selected tide pool and ownership of a fish discovered in such a pool becomes a fuzzy and potentially contentious point. Lastly, private or public property, herons, pelicans, ospreys and the like will take whatever they can catch. If you utilize a tide pool, just keep watch and stick close to your catch.

For privacy, RESTOP has a portable sanitation system (RESTOP.com).

CHAPTER 7

Natural Bait

Buying bait at the shop is a time-honored way to start the day. Also it's a good way to score local tips and insight from the staff. On the flipside, catching and preparing your own bait can be fun and rewarding. Show a first-timer how to catch their own bait and they'll watch that rod a lot closer when it's time to fish.

Snooping around tide pools and turning over rocks and oyster clumps reveals an amazingly diverse world of forage species. Young anglers often find this particularly delightful. Just make sure you A) protect your hands with gloves, B) know what you're grabbing and C) avoid reaching where you can't see your fingers. With all marine resources, check local regulations for size, season or bag limits, as well as any restrictions on harvest methods.

Snooping around tide pools and turning over rocks and oyster clumps reveals an amazingly diverse world of forage species.

Shallow shoreline areas reveal lots of places for bait species to hide. Right, telltale signs of a fiddler crab colony.

Bait Gathering Options

Call 'em mole crabs or sand fleas, these little guys are candy for several surf species.

Flea Finders

Mole crabs (a.k.a. "sand crabs" or sand fleas) make their home in the shallow surf and often tumble onto the sand when a receding wave leaves them exposed. As they dig back into the sand, water breaks around them and leaves a distinctive V-wake. Anglers quick enough to reach crabs before they burrow too deeply can grab a few fresh baits by hand. Otherwise, a sand flea rake with its aluminum teeth protruding from the edge of an angled catch basket makes the job easier. You'll find greater concentrations of sand fleas by wading about shin deep and raking the bottom. Wave action washes sand and shell grit through the mesh and leaves your fresh bait wriggling in the bottom.

Diligent use of a sand flea rake will reward anglers with one of the most effective baits in Southern waters.

Florida angler David Gill uses wave action to help filter sand fleas from their habitat.

The orange eggs of fresh sand fleas attract lots of bites. Hook these baits in the edge of the shell.

Net Gains

Cast a net over sardines, finger mullet, menaden or whatever's running through the surf and the indigenous forage gives you the benefit of fishing with what local predators naturally seek. Match your mesh size to the area's common baitfish and stick with a net diameter you can throw while standing in waist-deep water. If water depth prevents a sufficient back swing, stand at a 90-degree angle to where you'll throw the net, spin counterclockwise to build momentum (clockwise for lefties) and release the net at the proper alignment. Careful with your footing, especially in rough waves, or you might end up netting yourself. Keep a 5-gallon bucket of sea water nearby for shuttling live baits to your aerated bait tank.)

A net full of mullet gives this angler plenty of bait for a day of surf fishing at the beach.

Castnetters wade out to where the bait swims to load up nets, which they drag to the beach to unload.

Shiny Snares

A string of small gold-hooks, often dressed with quills and anchored by a lead weight—the "sabiki" rig—tempts baitfish into snapping at what resembles their tiny forage. It's mostly a boater's tool, but pier anglers can quickly gather fresh baits a few at a time without the burden of managing a net load of livies. In a calm surf, you might try rigging a sabiki under a cork with just a split shot at the end of the string. This enables you to take your shots at passing bait schools without the rig quickly dropping to the bottom. Note that trying this in heavy surf quickly becomes a lesson in futility, as wave action tangles the rig.

From crustaceans to mollusks, the surf zone attracts predators with a variety of forage options.

Toss handfuls of oyster shell grit into the surf and the wafting scent will establish your area as a potential feeding zone.

Fresh clam offers a tempting bait for many species of fish roaming the surf, but check local regulations before taking any on beaches.

Receding waves reveal an assortment of shellfish digging back into the sand.

DigThose Bivalves

From New Jersey to the Pacific Northwest, the various clams found on low tide mudflats certainly make a nice dinner, but they also yield excellent bait for striped bass, redfish, black drum, and many other surf feeders. Likewise, oysters common to seawalls, pier pilings and coastal creeks offer not only bait but a nifty chum option. Shuck the oysters and then use the top edge of a hammer to crush the shells into smelly grit inside a 5-gallon bucket. Toss handfuls of the shell grit into the surf and the wafting scent will establish your area as a potential feeding zone. Always check local regulations before taking shellfish.

Pump It Up

Ghost shrimp common to the Northern Gulf of Mexico and California burrow into soft mud where they dig meandering tunnels that make them tough to extract with shovels. Anglers aware of this crustacean's excellent bait value extract them with a handheld pump that looks something like a giant turkey baster.

Photo credit: Texas Parks and Wildlife Dept., Brenda Bo

Fooling Fiddlers

Find a tidal beach near marsh grass or a mangrove shoreline and you'll find loads of those audacious little crabs that wave their oversized claws at one another. Redfish, pompano, sheepshead, black drum, croakers and even trout will gobble fiddlers every chance they get, but for us clumsy two-legged predators, catching these burrowing crabs requires planning. On low tide, locate an active fiddler beach (lots of tiny sand balls indicates fresh burrowing activity), lay a window screen next to a densely populated area and scatter bits of cut shrimp or fish meal over the net. On the edge opposite the side from which you'll approach, bury several coffee cans at beach level.

Fiddlers don't like wasting their low-tide feeding period, so once you leave they'll quickly emerge, discover the free chow and crowd the screen. Once you've attracted enough crabs, dash forward to lift the screen and shake the fiddlers into a bucket. Those quick enough to exit the screen tumble into the secondary trap (coffee cans).

A live fiddler hooked in the carapace will delight redfish, sheepshead and many other surf species.

Capturing a bucket of fiddler crabs is no easy task, but the benefit justifies the effort.

Locate a tidal beach near marsh grass or a mangrove shoreline and you'll find loads of those audacious little crabs.

Rig It Right

Stronger surf conditions will require a heavier weight to hold your rig in position.

Natural bait rigging—live or dead—offers plenty of room for customization and situation-specific innovation. The following list offers a starting point with rigs of varying complexity that will cover the common surf-fishing scenarios. You'll find most designs online (specific sites noted where appropriate), while local tackle shop staff can show you how to tie those most relevant for your area.

Consider the target species and the day's conditions when selecting a surf rig.

Fish Finder with Sinker Slide

A pyramid or bank sinker clips to a plastic sleeve that slips onto the main line. This allows a fish to take the bait without immediately feeling any resistance. (Braided lines can cut through standard plastic slides, so use a nylon slide with braid.)

A sinker slide allows the weight to move freely along the leader.

Fish Finder with Leader Slide

The main leader threads through one ring of a swivel tied to the hook leader. A sinker clips to a duolock snap at the end of the main leader.

Redfish are one of the many species that a fish finder rig can help you locate.

The old reliable fish finder rig offers multiple configurations for various scenarios.

Fish Finder with 3-Way Swivel

Maintains a constant spacing relationship between main line, hook arm and weight arm. Good pier option.

A three-way swivel creates a bottom rig with the hook and weight set at fixed lengths.

Knocker Rig

A slip sinker slides freely on the leader and "knocks" against the hook. This keeps your rig compact and minimizes snagging around jetties, rocks and pier pilings.

The position of a rig's weight influences its performance.

A knocker rig is a good one to use when casting live bait.

Carolina Rig

Use light versions for small species like California surf perch or heavier rigs with chunk bait for red drum, striped bass, etc.

Lighter versions of the Carolina rig are popular for presenting natural baits in calm surf.

Owen Lupton Rig

An egg sinker flanked by red beads is secured 3 to 5 inches above a circle hook with crimps placed on the leader. The short leader ensures that the hook sets quickly so a redfish has minimal opportunity to spit the bait.

Creative rig design helps anglers achieve proper presentations.

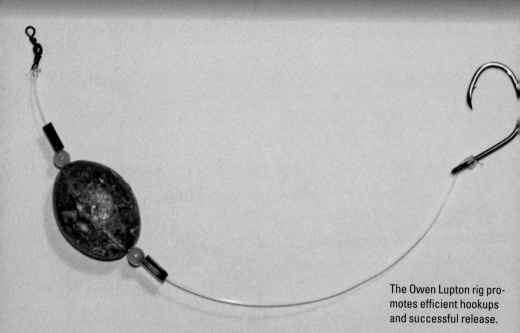

The Owen Lupton rig promotes efficient hookups and successful release.

Modified Owen Lupton Rig

If the fish seem to shy way from the weight n the leader, replace with a sinker slide, lso secured 3 to 5 nches above the hook vith crimps. Clipping pyramid sinker to the ide provides a little eparation (from Spud Voodward).

Moving the weight from the leader to a sinker slide makes the modified Owen Lupton rig less intimidating for wary fish.

Anchovy Imitator

Carolina rig with inch-long strip of squid on a small circle hook. Current lifts and wiggles the bait strip nd mimics a small anchovy or other baitfish. Good way to catch blue runners and other baitfish under iers for kingfish or shark duties.

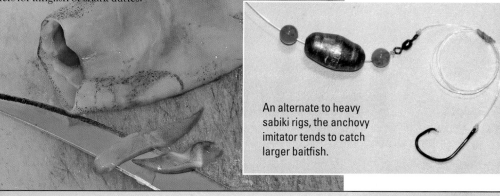

An alternate to heavy sabiki rigs, the anchovy imitator tends to catch larger baitfish.

Flounder Float Rig

Essentially a Carolina rig with a float and beads secured with crimps pout 3 inches above the hook. The float keeps your bait off the bottom and away from aggressive crabs.

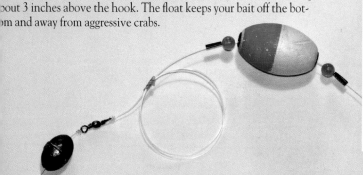

Flounder Fanatic Bottom Hook

Specialized flat weight molded with a laterally-oriented hook that keeps the bait at mouth level for flounder. (http://www.flounderfanatic.com/).

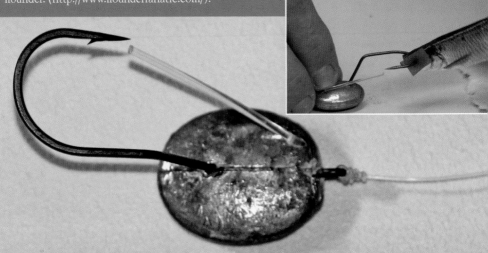

Given their flat bodies and bottom-oriented feeding style, flounder have inspired a variety of specialized rigs.

Bucktail Flounder Rig

Tie your main line to the top ring of a 3-way swivel, attach a snap for sinker connection to one of the side rings and a 12- to 18-inch leader to the other. Add a spinner blade flanked by red beads and a bucktail skirt to the leader before snelling to a kahle hook. The bucktail adds visual appeal that attracts attention to your bait—squid or mullet strip or a live minnow (Joemalat.com).

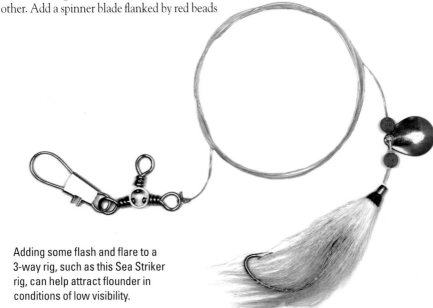

Adding some flash and flare to a 3-way rig, such as this Sea Striker rig, can help attract flounder in conditions of low visibility.

ouble Dropper Rig

Dropper arms looped to circle or kahle hooks are
ssed with plastic or brass beads to attract pom-
no, whiting, redfish, trout, spot, croakers, etc.

Double Dropper with Floats

Some days, pompano will want their baits
off the bottom and adding small pill floats
ahead of each hook elevates the presentation.
(Try one hook with a float and one without to
determine the day's preference.)

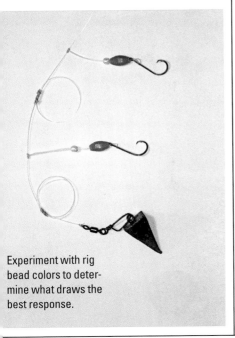

Experiment with rig
bead colors to deter-
mine what draws the
best response.

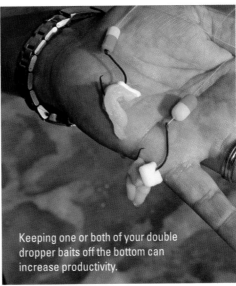

Keeping one or both of your double
dropper baits off the bottom can
increase productivity.

igs with double droppers allow you to vary your baits and presentations.

inger Mullet Rig

A wire stem with a line tie holds a float at one end and a detachable double hook at the other. Remove
e hook, run the wire through the bait's mouth and out the back end. Reattach the hook and pull the
re back forward to snug the twin point against the mullet.

The finger mullet rig's cork keeps it higher in the
water column for better visibility.

Floating Sabiki

Suspend a gold-hook rig (hooks tipped with shrimp) under a cork. Great way to snare live baits for heavy surf rods. Also very productive when silver trout schools run the beach.

Effective for catching live bait, sabiki rigs also hook clothing and fingers, so handle with care.

Keep your sabiki under control by first attaching the weight and then pulling out the branches one at a time.

Fireball Rig

Similar to the Double Dropper with Floats, this one uses larger, round floats—usually brightly colored—ahead of long-shank hooks that hold cut bait. Often called "Bluefish Rigs" for the species they commonly attract (Joemalat.com).

Big and bold, the Fireball rig's high-vis floats are sure to attract attention.

Double Bucktail

Rig two bucktails on dropper loops, but skip the surf weight you'd rig with double bait hooks. (Use a heavier bucktail on the bottom so it leads the cast.) Tip the bucktails with strips of cut squid or mullet, or live minnows (Joemalat.com).

Double bucktail rigs are usually tipped with natural bait, but they're also effective bare.

Replacing traditional lead surf weights with bucktails is a creative configuration.

Steel Leader Shark Rig

Designs vary, but the object is to keep a big, toothy fish from biting or tail-whipping its way to freedom. An effective leader must be at least as long as the shark you hope to catch.

Steel leaders long enough to span the body of a large shark are essential for withstanding incredible biting power.

Mackerel Rig

Nothing more than an 18-inch wire leader and a treble hook, this rig enables you to cast live baitfish or shrimp towar mackerel or bluefish that run close to a pier or jetty. Connect mainline to wire leader with a tiny black swivel (no shiny hardware to attract bites).

S. Tokunaga's Floating Rig

A barrel swivel links main line to leader and a snap swivel slipped onto the leader clips to a stem float that keeps the rig high in the surf. Affix a piece of plastic tubing to the stem and insert a small light stick for night fishing. (tokunagastore.com)

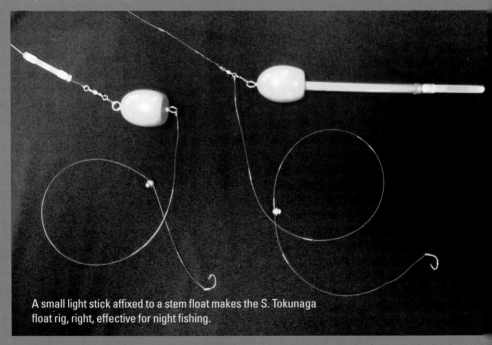

A small light stick affixed to a stem float makes the S. Tokunaga float rig, right, effective for night fishing.

A double dropper rig with floats tempted this whiting on Florida's New Smyrna Beach.

Surf fishing rigs can be simple or complex, but there's a design that works for whatever you want to catch.

Crafty with Crustaceans

Not many surf species will turn down a shrimp dinner, so rig appropriately for the scenario.

For a mid-depth presentation, drift a shrimp across the strike zone beneath a popping cork.

Being a shrimp—now, that has to rank at least top-5 on the "Worst Jobs" list. But what's bad for the crustacean is good for the angler because whether it's the brown, white, pink or ghost variety, just about every fish in the surf will eat every shrimp they can find. Catching those fish, however, requires proper rigging, so use a style befitting your scenario and objective. Options include:

Float It

For a mid-depth presentation, drift your shrimp across a strike zone by hanging it beneath a popping cork, or a clacking cork rig. Floats—particularly weighted models—increase casting distance, while chugging them across the surface mimics topside feeding to attract trout and other predators. (Good tactic for calm, shallow surf; as well as piers and jetties.)

Cutting shrimp into pieces makes your bait last longer, while improving your hookups.

Keep your shrimp higher in the water column and give it a chugging sound with a popping-cork rig.

Head Shot

Insert the hook at the base of the horn and run it through the side of the shell so it comes out next to the horn, facing forward. This ensures an in-line cast and a straight retrieve track. In colder weather, head hook a shrimp with a 1/8- to ¼-ounce jig for targeted casting and slow bottom presentations. (Avoid poking the dark spot in the shrimp's head. That's the brain and accidental contact kills your bait.)

When you need to make long casts with a shrimp, hook it through the tail for a more aerodynamic package.

End Game

A shrimp's thick, muscular tail offers a solid hooking point that withstands the pressure of a snappy cast needed for maximum distance. For redfish, trout and flounder—fish that typically gobble baits whole—hook your live shrimp through the first joint of the tail with the hook facing aft. Pierce the underside of the shell, as opposed to going through the soft joint for a more solid hook placement. Before hooking, pinch off the tail fins to releases more scent and minimize wind resistance.

For greater casting distance, insert a jig's hook through the shrimp's tail, bottom-to-top and space it forward so the lead head hides between the tail fins. This is a good arrangement for pitching shrimp between pier pilings or any tight quarters requiring a streamlined presentation. Another option: Replace the jig with a hook and a split shot positioned next to the knot.

If pinfish or other bait-stealers continue pecking too much of your bait, pinch off the shrimp's tail fins and thread the tail onto the hook or jighead. This minimizes the amount of shrimp hanging loose and increases your chances of hooking whatever bites. Use a longshank hook for jumbo shrimp.

(Above and below) Threading a shrimp tail-first onto your jig or hook helps alleviate the annoyance of pinfish and other bait-stealers and gives the shrimp a natural, backward-jumping action on retrieval.

Ready and Reachable

A few creative options for holding your natural bait

Not Too Many Minnows

If you use live baitfish for surf wading, you'll burn a lot of time returning to your aerated bait tank, or your anchored boat. Towing a flow-through bait bucket tied to your waist extends your range, but don't overfill the bucket. Even with ventilated sides for even water flow, cramped interior space stresses live baits and greatly reduces their flashing attraction and longevity.

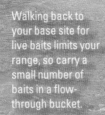

Walking back to your base site for live baits limits your range, so carry a small number of baits in a flow-through bucket.

You can secure the bait container to your belt or waist with heavy monofilament or fluorocarbon.

Cozy in Coquina

Florida surf angler David Gill keeps his live sand fleas in a plastic bin half filled with coquina—the dense mix of tiny shell fragments common to North Florida beaches. Gill uses only dry coquina because it absorbs the crabs' waste and neutralizes chemicals that can kill bait. If he'll use them for multiple days, he'll remove the baits and dry the coquina after each trip by sticking the container in the microwave for about 20 seconds. (Let the coquina cool before returning the baits.)

Dry coquina is a good environment to keep sand fleas alive in for longer periods.

In the Bag

Lastly, while those airtight, freezer proof and dishwasher safe food storage containers make handy containers for dead shrimp, clam strips and cut squid, you'll also have to march back to your base of operations each time you need a bait reload. Maximize your fishing time by carrying several pieces of bait in a Ziploc bag stuffed into your shirt or pants pocket. (It should go without saying, but make sure that bag's shut securely or you'll find a most unpleasant odor in your clothing.)

This angler keeps a selection of baits in a Ziploc bag in his shirt pocket.

Chilled Shrimp

Lacking an aerated live well, try this old Homosassa, Florida trick for keeping shrimp alive: Fill the bottom of small cooler with a generous layer of ice, fold two paper grocery bags to fit the cooler's interior and soak it with saltwater. Lay one of the saturated bags over the ice, line up your shrimp single file and lay the other bag over top. The ice lowers the shrimp's metabolism, while the draining saltwater maintains stable conditions. When it's time to fish, just hook your shrimp as normal and a few seconds in the warmer water perks them back to flipping order.

Heavy Thoughts

Lead weights anchoring your natural bait rigs come in various styles that primarily address bottom composition and surf conditions. The basic sinker styles include:

Pyramid

An angled form (three- and four-sided models) holds rigs in place for stationary presentations. Best used in sandy areas.

Bank

Basically an elongated teardrop shape with a molded eye at the top, a bank sinker is your choice for uneven bottom (rocks, shells) because its smooth profile resists snagging.

Storm
(aka hurricane or Hatteras)

Top end similar to a pyramid weight, but the lower portion narrows, typically in a rounded shape. Storm weights provide greater holding strength than comparable pyramids.

Egg (aka slip sinker)

Oval shape with a hole through its lengthwise center, this weight rolls in the surf for a more dynamic presentation. Also, the line-through design allows a fish to move off with a larger bait without immediately feeling resistance.

Disc (aka pancake)

Round or slightly teardrop shaped with flat sides (line tie, line-through or in-line style), this weight slides across the bottom for a stealthy presentation. Commonly used for flounder rigs.

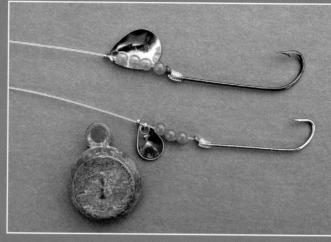

Sputnik

This oblong weight sports four metal legs that dig into the bottom to hold securely in strong surf. The angled legs snap free from their locked position when the angler applies sufficient pressure. Adjustable leg tension enables you to tune your weight for prevailing surf conditions.

The missile version offers a more advanced system than the Sputnik with a plastic base with leg locks and plastic leg supports. A similar style, the "spider" weight typically has four wire arms molded into a short lead body with a stem and line tie extending from the top end.

Whether you surf fish from the beach, a pier or a jetty, you'll do well to learn a handful of basic rigs that you can modify for specific scenarios.

Building surf rigs in advance will let you maximize your fishing time and make the most of being the first one on a spot.

CHAPTER 8

Artificial Baits

Natural baits require less physical effort, but you're investing much time and trust in each presentation. With artificial lures, several casts may precede each hookup, but any given cast could draw a strike, so periods of rapid productivity often reward diligence. Here's a look at the common surf lure selection applicable for everything from striped bass in the Northeast, to trout in the Texas surf.

Natural baits are usually an easy sell, but surf anglers who take on the challenge of fooling big fish with artificials often reap impressive rewards.

Predators like snook
are particularly
vulnerable to
artificials at night.

Topwaters

Tossing topwaters into the dim light of sundown can deliver incredibly violent strikes.

A good selection of sizes, shapes and colors will keep your topwater bite going.

Surface lures appeal to many kinds of fish, especially predators given to corralling and driving baitfish top-side. Forage species may at times breach the surface by flipping, leaping or skipping, but once predators like striped bass, mackerel, bonito, bluefish, trout or cobia lock onto a food source, it's usually just a matter of time.

Walking style topwaters – those retrieved with a side-to-side motion – resemble baitfish meandering at the surface where opportunistic predators keep frequent watch for such vulnerable targets. Notwithstanding the big bait-big fish generalization, surf denizens may at times just boil on your large topwaters or shun them altogether.

Surface baits add a key element to any tackle box.

Topwater baits take advantage of the natural predatory instinct to pin baitfish against the surface.

If conditions seem right for topwater action – especially if you observe surface feeding – try downsizing baits.

Tip: If a fish misses your topwater in calm, clear conditions, "kill" the bait and let it sit for several seconds. Trout and other predators given to topwater strikes often watch what they perceive as a wounded bait for any signs of movement. Give it a 10-count and expect a foaming follow-up strike the second you resume the action. If you don't get a take, walk it home and start over.

In big surf with lots of turbulence and white water, predators respond mostly to a bait's motion and vibrations. However, sound remains a common tool for fish attraction, so keep a few rattling baits in your mix – particularly for shallow and calmer surf scenarios. Note that lure manufacturers use various materials for bodies and rattles to create subtle low-pitch or more frantic high-pitch sounds. Weather and light conditions can affect what the fish want based on their level of aggression, but the preference may change throughout the day, so pay attention to what works in which conditions.

Topwater poppers or chuggers are floating baits with flat or concave faces. These rely on water resistance to create the chugging, spitting and sputtering commotion that fish like.

Such noisemakers can produce in calm conditions and high visibility, but they're particularly effective when some combination of low light and rough water decrease visibility and the fish need a little help locating baits.

The Gibbs Canal Special and Strike Pro's Ron Arra series Surf Pro Flat Bottom Pencil both feature a flat belly for optimal control in rough surf. Situation-specific versions of their round-bellied models, these baits track better in conditions that would roll a rounded plug too much.

Surface swimmers like the Gibbs Casting Swimmer and Creek Chub Surfster combine elements of the walking and popping topwater styles. Sporting shallow angled lips, these baits are made primarily for surface swimming with

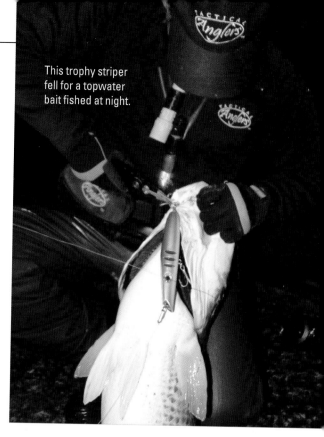

This trophy striper fell for a topwater bait fished at night.

enticing back-and-forth motion to mimic the larger forage that big stripers, redfish, and bluefish seek. In southern waters, snook and tarpon might mistake these plugs for meandering mullet.

In calm conditions, retrieve with a casual saunter and impart the occasional sharp twitch to make the lure surge and splash like a startled baitfish. In rough water, you'll want to maintain contact with the bait by speeding up the retrieve on the front of a wave and slowing down on the backside.

Walking-style topwaters rely on a steady cadence to tempt fish.

Subsurface

When fish shy away from surface presentations, they'll often respond better to a subsurface bait.

When fish snub topwaters, dig deeper to reach fish feeding below the waves. Used as "search baits" or for targeting particular areas (bait schools, blow-ups, bird activity, etc.), subsurface lures also make good follow-ups to missed topwater strikes – something to keep in mind when wading with a spare rod tucked in your gear belt.

Whether it's big stripers, bruiser reds or smaller surf fish like trout, mackerel and puppy drum, a variety of subsurface bait styles enable you to address various situational factors. With suspending and slow sinking plugs, you simply cast to the target zone and work the bait at the desired depth. Short-lipped floater/divers will sit topside until you pull them below the surface with steady reeling or sharp downward jerks. These plugs, sometimes called "rip baits," are designed for a more peppy display than suspenders and slow sinkers.

When picking a subsurface bait, first consider your depth. Making follow-up casts to stripers in a deep New England channel, or snook off the end of Florida's Sebastian Inlet jetty merits a larger and deeper reaching lure than sight fishing for speckled trout in 2-3 feet of calm Texas beach brine. Forage size also factors here and fortunately, the lineup of subsurface lures includes a plug t match just about any baitfish profile.

Also consider exactly what you're trying to imitate. Are schools of small baitfish clustering on the edge of an outer sandbar that you can walk to on low tide? A suspending twitchbait would work well here. Are trout and other predators launching nocturnal attacks in the pier's light rings? Try casting a slow sinker upcu rent and bringing it down through the lighted area. (If you notice the fish attacking higher in the water, switch to a suspending bait.). In ope: water or along the edge of a jetty, rock groin or any other hard line structure, frantic baitfish activity indicates nearby predators. Work that shallow diving rip bait around the perimeter of the melee and you'll likely attract the attentior of something with an appetite.

Swimbaits, as the name implies, swim with n additional "action" needed – just throw 'em ou

and reel 'em back. Hard body baits like Sebile's Magic Swimmer, Storm's Kickin' Stick and Strike Pro's Needle Jointed rely on segmented body designs for their realistic motion, while most soft swimmers get their action from a tail design that wiggles and kicks on the retrieve. The latter can be fished either on weighted or unweighted swimbait hooks or lead heads. Some swimmers like Tsunami's Holographic Swim Shad and Berkley's Powerbait Swimbait are made with built-in lead heads. DOA's BFL combines a soft body with a jointed frame.

r depth when
g a
ce lure.

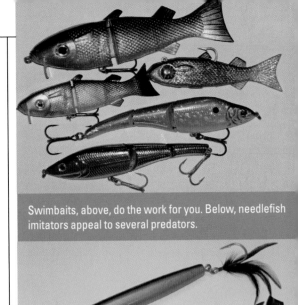

Swimbaits, above, do the work for you. Below, needlefish imitators appeal to several predators.

Shallow diving plugs, left and right, deliver a peppy display that appeals to predators. When the fish turn picky, you'll appreciate a diverse selection of sizes and colors.

Jigs

A light jighead offers an adjustable platform for various plastic tails.

eadhead jigs offer a versatile tool for wading and sight casting, probing jetty perimeters or bouncing around pier pilings. Keep several sizes available for various depths and wind conditions and try different shapes – paddle tails, curl tails, soft jerkbaits, etc. – to dial in what the fish want. Scented synthetic baits like Berkley Gulp! Shrimp can be very effective on a jighead.

Banana-shaped jigs made with weighted hook shanks are great for pompano, as are round or bullet head jigs with short nylon skirts. With banana jigs, rigging a small pink fly to the eye with a split ring enhances the attraction.

One of the all-time favorites across the angling spectrum, bucktails or "hair" jigs benefit from a breathing effect that adds lifelike appearance. The hair contracts on forward motion and expands whe you pause the jig. Popular in various sizes for surf favorites including striped bass, salmon, cobia, bluefi trout, redfish, flounder and halibut, bucktails produ well when fished bare, fitted with a curly tail grub c tipped with a live eel, finger mullet or bonito strip.

Synthetic Shrimp

Use a slow presentation with occasional twitches to mimic the authentic crustacean sau ter marked by evasive dashes. Smaller sizes mal great sight-fishing baits for trout, redfish, flounc and snook; while larger models will tempt a var ety of species from cobia to tarpon when worke through pier lights or allowed to drift with the tide past a jetty's outer edge.

The banana-shaped pompano jig, and other jig shapes, appeal to a variety of species.

Versatile and easy to cast, jigs allow you to offer mulitple "looks."

Spoons

The weighted spoon rig is effective for catching mackerel and other minnow eaters from piers.

When in doubt, throw a spoon. This timeless angling axiom works for two main reasons: First, most spoons cast like a bullet and punch through even a stiff wind. Second, and most significant, the spoon's wobbling, flashing appearance impersonates forage fish just about anywhere you go. Each region has its local favorite, but you can't go wrong with classics like Luhr-Jensen Krocodile, Acme Kastmaster, Hopkins, Tony Accetta and Johnson Sprite. Top colors are silver and gold, but chartreuse produces on brighter days, while black spoons offer the right silhouette in low light. Spoons with accent colors like the Luhr-Jensen Laxee UV Bright series provide more visual stimulus in murky water.

A popular trick for tempting Spanish mackerel, bluefish and others fond of the fast and flashy involves rigging a bucktail or tinsel jig ahead of a spoon on a wire leader system. Bomber offers a premade version with a metal-head tinsel attractor over a 3/0 hook and a Capt. Action spoon trailing on a separate length of coated single strand No. 6 wire leader.

Small silver spoons are one of the top baits for Spanish mackerel.

Luhr Jensen Krocodile spoons, top, and Williamson Gomame jigs, bottom, cast well in the wind.

Flashy and efficient, spoons really shine in windy conditions.

Spoons appeal to all predators fond of eating small baitfish.

Whatever you throw, consider these following points when selecting and preparing your lures.

There are many varieties of line and leader, each specific for your type of fishing.

Line

Braid's superior sensitivity offers optimal lure control and the ability to consistently set the hook from a distance. Conversely, braid's zero stretch can inadvertently pull the bait away from a fish, so if you pr braid, let the rod load up before going hard on the fish.

Leaders

A fluorocarbon leader adds a nearly invisible buffe between your bait and main line—a necessary step in clear conditions. Too much fluoro leader can mar a walking topwater bait's presentation by pulling down the nose and impeding its side-to-side action. Drop y bait next to you and examine its posture—if the nose dips too much, shorten your leader.

Knots

In most cases, a loop knot works best, as it allows optimal lure motion. In the less common instances where you may want a rigid connection (i.e. hopping a jig across rocks), go with an improved clinch or Palomar knot. With single strand stainless steel wire leaders, use a haywire twist at the lure end and link wire to main line with an

Albright Special or haywire the leader's top end small black swivel and then tie the main line her

Anglers seeking big sharks in the surf use he duty leaders made of cabled wire typically secu with crimping sleeves – a design strategy that a works well with the lighter wire leaders used fo bluefish, Spanish mackerel, kingfish and smalle sharks. However, knottable wire lea material like American Fishing Wire' Surflon Micro Supreme, TyGer Lead and Knot 2 Kinky Nickel Titanium Wir enable you to tie a wire l er to hooks, lures, flies a main line just as you wou with monofilament or flu rocarbon. Optimal flexibi no memory and less stre than monofilaments yiel superior presentation th resists toothy jaws. Also nixing crimps, swivels ar snaps can help convince tackle-shy fish in conditi of higher visibility.

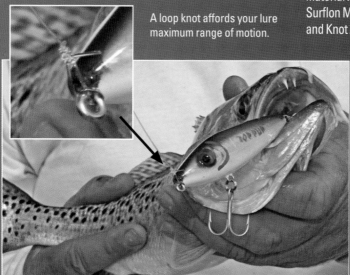

A loop knot affords your lure maximum range of motion.

Colors

In turbulent surf, fish won't get more than a glimpse of your lure, so precise colors and scale patterns probably aren't as crucial as they are in scenarios of higher visibility. Nevertheless, the basics of color selection – brighter, more vivid colors during sunny periods; darker patterns for dim conditions – always provide a good starting point. From there, "match-the-hatch" will guide your decisions. Does the local forage have a black back, or is it more of a greenish tint? Any spots or stripes?

Given the flashy flanks of most forage fish, baits with silver or gold sides consistently produce, while red accents mimic a wounded and therefore vulnerable baitfish. At night, baits with fluorescent "glow" finishes get plenty of attention, especially around pier lights.

A selection of colors, like these scented Logic Lures, enables you to match conditions and fish temperament.

Size

Distance vs. stealth – it's the grand dilemma of lure selection. On one hand, a heavier plug generally allows greater casting distance, thereby keeping you farther from your quarry and minimizing intrusion. However, if that big plug drops with such a splash that it sends the fish packing, of what use was that lengthy cast?

There's no one-size-fits-all pattern for lure presentation, but keen observation of conditions and fish response will help you dial in the particulars. First, know that fish are keenly aware of their vulnerability in clear water and sunny skies. When visibility's high, downsizing artificials can help you tempt wary fish. Dimmer conditions usually see an uptick in aggression, so a full size lure could be just the deal.

The rougher the water, the more lure splash the fish will tolerate. Indeed, when an incoming tide and windy conditions stir up a moody surf, you'll actually need that big splash and subsequent noisy presentation to help the fish locate your bait. Conversely, in calmer scenarios shift the emphasis to subtlety. Ask a Florida snook fisherman how long it takes those linesiders to vanish when a full-size topwater crashes over their heads. Any time surf fish move through placid, clear waters you'll want to lead them with a light jig, a small swimbait, a scaled-down surface plug.

Keep a selection of bait sizes handy, including tiny ones, right.

On the Fly

Throughout most coastal waters, flies that impersonate the dominant local baitfish will serve you well, while crustacean imitators are a good bet around any rocky structures and the sandy beaches where bonefish, permit, corbina, croakers or sand perch patrol. Environment and surf conditions dictate tackle size, so if you're wading the sandy shallows of a relatively calm beach in Southern California, Florida's Atlantic Coast, or maybe one of Georgia's barrier islands, an 8-weight rod is plenty for your smaller nearshore species. Take on the big surf and rocky coastlines where northeastern stripers, bluefish and false albacore roam and you'll need a longer rod of 9- to 10-weight. Line should match what you're throwing and where you throw it. Ask yourself these questions: Does the fly imitate forage the swims the water column or something that crawls across the bottom? How will surf conditions affect my line's sink rate? Address these key points and choose a line that delivers a realistic presentation.

Tackle selection and tactics will vary with habitat, conditions and targeted species, but Capt. Rick Grassett, an inshore guide and certified fly instructor based in Sarasota, Fla., offered a basic tutorial that will help guide decision making in most any surf-fishing scenario.

Rod Length: Most fly rods are 9' which are adequate and are what I use. Since there isn't much structure and most fish aren't large (3 or 4-pounds), 7 and 8-wt rods are fine. I might use a 9-wt for casting larger flies or in wind.

Line/Leader: I prefer a clear intermediate sink tip line, which will get your fly below any wave action. If there isn't much wave action, a floating line with a 12-foot leader will also work fine.

Presentations: I am usually sight casting for snook in the surf, although other species are encountered. I usually stand on the sand a few

Wading the shallow surf with fly gear offers great sight-fishing opportunities for tasty species like flounder

Above, baitfish patterns with lead eyes will reach beneath the waves. Below, a stripping basket facilitates line management.

feet from the edge of the water where the beach slopes up slightly for the best visibility.

Usually the fly is cast ahead of an approaching fish either quartering away from the fish or perpendicular to the fish. A perpendicular cast must be timed perfectly so it meets the fish's path at the right time. Don't cast beyond the line the fish is swimming on or you may spook them if the fly comes toward the fish from the other side.

Usually flies are stripped with short strips and sped up to trigger a strike when you get a follow. Sometimes stripping will need to be varied-if short strips spook fish or don't trigger strikes, I would try a longer more steady stripping action.

Fighting/Landing:
Usually I'm fishing the surf in calm conditions since I'm sight casting rather than blind casting and rough conditions yield poor visibility. If I were fighting a fish in rough surf, the same techniques would apply as in other conditions, rod tip low and to the side to apply the most pressure. You may need to raise your rod tip

above the level of the waves if the surf is significant. I usually slide them up on the beach on their belly to land them so wave action can help.

(When it comes to fly selection, Grassett said there's no better rule of thumb than "match the hatch" by duplicating size and profile of indigenous forage. However, in turbulent surf conditions, he suggests upsizing.)

In rough surf I would probably use a larger, wider profile fly or a more heavily weighted fly. Since the water will be more silted, a larger fly may be easier to find and a heavier fly may be less affected by wave action.

Many of the species available to fly fishermen will run very close to shore.

A Fresh Water Approach

Many of the baits used by fresh-water bass anglers will also produce in surf habitat.

Inshore anglers seeking trout, redfish and flounder know well the crossover potential found in their freshwater tackle bags. Surf anglers will also find several traditional bass tactics effective in various scenarios. Here's a rundown of the likely candidates for double duty:

Crankbaits

Running along the bottom, kicking up dirt and bumping off hard structure – the same raucous displays that tempt largemouth bass deliver a different look that might also interest redfish, trout, black drum, stripers and other surf zone predators. Depending on depth, try medium to deep divers.

Fan casting the target area may be a good search strategy, but once you dial in an active area, cast parallel to the bank if you can stand in that preferred depth, or diagonally if not. The key is keeping that lure running through the strike zone as long as possible.

Pier anglers can leverage deeper diving cranks to reach peripheral rocks or reefs. If the target's beyond your casting range, let the outgoing tide float your bait past the structure, hold your rod low and crank fast to pull the lure close enough to tick off the hard surface. (Hold on tightly, as a lazy grip can cost you a rod.)

Designed to deflect off cover, squarebill crankbaits offer a good way to probe those gnarled driftwood skeletons or nearshore rocks. Strikes usually occur as the bait bounces off a solid surface so fish close and make lots of contact. Lipless crankbaits emit lots of sound and vibration to attract aggressive fish. (Very effective in conditions of lower visibility, or any time you can reach a school of baitfish under attack.)

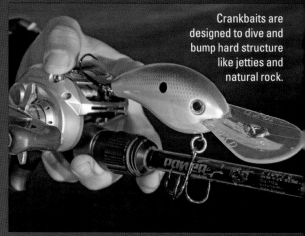

Crankbaits are designed to dive and bump hard structure like jetties and natural rock.

Suspending Jerkbait

Vulnerability gets baitfish eaten, and suspending or slow-sinking jerkbaits/slashbaits are hard to resist. For effective presentations, make a long cast, reel fast and crank hard to "jerk" or "rip" the bait down into the water column and then let it sit. Follow with varying cadences of twitching and pausing to mimic a wounded baitfish.

Hang a jerkbait along the edge of bridge lights, suspend it over submerged rocks or twitch and pause it in shallow, clear surf where trout feed. In sand shallows, don't be surprised to find a flounder or halibut rising to grab the easy prey.

Football Head Jig

The oblong head rumbles over rocks and shells with less likelihood of snagging – a helpful benefit for bumping along jetties and natural rock. Also, the football design allows you to pause the jig without it tipping over for a good imitation of a foraging eel (when used with a slender plastic body).

Football heads can traverse uneven bottom with minimal snagging.

crossover bait is likely to interest trout, redfish, cobia, bluefish and mackerel. The latter two will mangle wire frames and shred skirts, so keep a couple of spares handy.

No one's suggesting we replace traditional surf tactics with a bass fisherman's tackle bag, but experimentation broadens repertoire. Some of these tactics closely mimic natural forage, while others just show the fish something different. Either way, plan on replacing stock treble hooks with corrosion-resistant saltwater grade models and washing your baits after their briny bath.

Umbrella Rig

This multi-armed bait school simulator traces its roots to coastal and offshore anglers seeking to tease up everything from striped bass to bluewater species like tuna, dolphin, wahoo and sailfish. Today's umbrella rig took the bass world by storm when its castable incarnation burst onto the scene in 2011. Innovation quickly followed with anglers trying all sorts of swimming plastic bodies on rigs of three to five arms, sometimes dressed with flasher blades. This heavy and cumbersome rig is best thrown from a relatively flat plane of the beach or shallow surf, as your field of presentation is less when worked from the elevated position of a pier or jetty. You'll also want to hold this one for calm conditions, as pulling this rig through big waves will feel like you're winding in a 5-gallon bucket.

Buzzbait

A wire frame sports a clacking blade over a hook dressed with a fish head and a pulsing skirt. Ripping this bold bait across the water's surface creates a frantic gurgling presentation that mimics fleeing baitfish skipping across the top. This

Complementing your traditional surf baits with freshwater lures expands your arsenal.

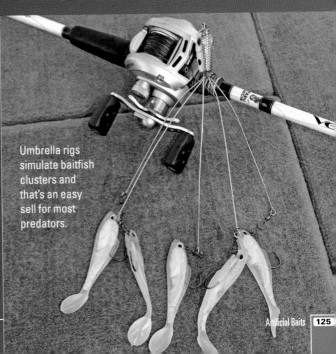

Umbrella rigs simulate baitfish clusters and that's an easy sell for most predators.

CHAPTER 9

New England

B oldly iconic is the image of New England surf anglers challenging wind-swept beaches and deftly negotiating treacherous rocks to fling huge lures into chilly waters teeming with striped bass. No doubt, when stripers pin bait schools against a shoreline, the resulting blitzes are nothing short of astounding. Anglers perched on rocks survey the furious feeds and fire hefty plugs toward the fracas.

Where cold waters wash rocky shores, New England anglers challenge the habitat as much as the fish they seek.

Whopper bluefish rank below stripers in glamor, but they lack not for fighting ability.

Precarious Positions

Between such heart-pounding windows of opportunity, striper fishermen stake out likely locations in top-tier strongholds such as Martha's Vineyard and Nantucket Island, Gloucester, Mass., the Cape Cod Canal (east entrance) and Nantasket Beach in Hull, Mass. (busy swimming beach during warm season, so night fishing is best). Elsewhere, New England Surf Fishing Club member Rick Jenkins likes Provincetown and Head of Meadow Beach (north end of Cape Cod), but his favorite striper destination is the west end of Cuttyhunk Island. Sitting about five miles south of New Bedford, Mass., at the southern end of the Elizabeth Islands chain, Cuttyhunk boasts a solid striper fishery steeped in local surf fishing club history. Mid-May-June and then Sept.-Oct. offers thrilling action on that distant western beach, but Jenkins said he's found the long hike from the pedestrian ferry dock at Cuttyhunk Pond (north end) well worth the effort.

A well-known regional regular, "Crazy" Alberto Knie spends his striper time from the north end of Long Island through the Cape Cod area. Knie said he fares best by targeting points, jetties, coves and back bays. Tides, he said—particularly the levels of each high and low—are critical to his planning, as the water level dictates fish positioning and that's obviously what positions fishermen.

Knie points out that tides grow stronger and coastal waters become cleaner as you progress northward from the Long Island Sound area. Wherever his extensive travel takes him, Knie

After capturing a sizeable striper, this angler still has to contend with the turbulent surf.

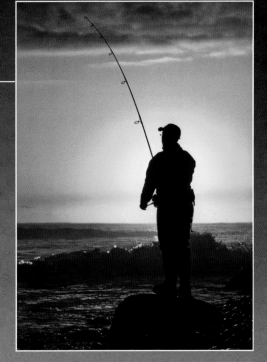

typically avoids the "town beaches" and instead gravitates to the more lightly-traveled perimeter areas where he looks for sand bars, mussel beds and rocky outcroppings as signs of good striper waters.

"Wind has a tremendous impact on your fishing and you can use wind to your advantage, particularly if you know there's a certain type of bait in the area," Knie said. "For example, menhaden (bunker) always swim against the wind so I generally go with whatever area is against the wind. I find it's very easy to locate fish from the shore with wind, and that goes for bluefish, as well as stripers. Wind in your face is always the best."

Calling himself "an opportunistic fisherman," Knie said that while he prefers plug casting for the mostly nocturnal feeding stripers, he'll play the cards he's dealt. Specializing in trophy stripers of 40-plus pounds, he devotes 70 percent of his fishing time to non-daylight hours. In the darkness, clean water presents the best opportunities for fish to locate an artificial. Conversely, dirty, stained or "chocolate" water will find him rigging for live bait or chunking presentations with porgies, bunker, herring or eels.

Off the beaches, Knie fishes natural baits on a fishfinder rig assembled with an 80- to 100-pound shock leader tied to a No. 10/0 Octopus-style hook and weighted with up to an 8-ounce pyramid sinker (egg sinkers for jetty fishing). Heavy conventional outfits with 80-pound braid enable him to launch heavy rigs into the holes, cuts and channels where stripers tend to gather. When the stripers run close to jetties or breakers, Knie will ditch the fish finder and freeline his baits to short-range targets on a No. 5/0 J-hook with a 50- to 80-pound leader.

Big stripers like this more than justify the effort they require.

Awash with equal parts ambiance and intrigue, nighttime often brings the best striper action.

Gear Up and Zip Up

Describing his standard armament, Knie said: "I use conventional reels and a 12-foot rod because of the heavier payload. In the areas I fish, we're targeting larger stripers and they like very rocky areas—anywhere they can break your line. It's easier to handle them on conventional tackle."

When daytime conditions favor artificials, Knie will throw a mix of 4- to 9-inch rubber shads (matched to local forage size), swimbaits and bucktails with curly tail trailers for sweeping the lower part of the water column. Popping plugs like his Tactical Angler Bomb Popper are his top choice—especially when stripers are visibly chasing bunker. At night, Knie targets the shadow lines of lighthouses, light poles and bridge lights with darters and needlefish, which mimic the slender baitfish that stripers love. For any artificials, Knie said diversity marks the effective presentation.

"A lot of people have a tendency to just cast and retrieve at a slow pace and most times you will catch fish," Knie said. "But I like to vary my retrieves. For example, when I'm using the darter, I always allow it to sweep with the cur-

rent. From time to time, when I'm retrieving at a nice, slow pace, I tend to pause it for a quick jerk just in case I have a follower. Then, I pick up the pace and repeat. When those big fish are finicky, they follow the bait and as soon as you pause it and twitch it, that's when they'll strike it."

On open beaches, Knie prefers a softer rod with a parabolic bend, which facilitates his power pendulum casting technique. On a rocky beach, where he needs to reach out and over the trouble spots, he likes the distance and precision of a fast-action graphite composite rod—also his choice for artificials. Whatever he throws, Knie said habitat determines leader length.

"If I'm fishing an open beach, the leader could be very short," he said. "If I'm fishing a jetty or a high, rocky area, it's all about the ability to land a fish by grabbing the leader, so it can go up to 5 feet. If I'm using natural bait on an open beach and I need to reach out there, I'll use a short leader with my fishfinder rig. Obviously, the shorter your leader, the more casting distance you'll get because it doesn't give you that propeller effect."

As New England Surf Fishing Club member Rick Jenkins notes, New England summers see plenty of days when the shorts-and-barefoot style works just fine off sandy beaches. Fall and early spring, however, are a different story. During warmer months, the truly motivated will gear up with wetsuits and fins, which enable them to swim out to isolated rocks affording solitude and access

After braving the big surf, this angler proudly hauls her catch to shore.

o deeper fish. From about June through September, Alberto Knie takes to the surf in a 5-millimeter wetsuit. After that, the water becomes too cold o tolerate and he'll stick to the shoreline with chest waders, a dry top and plenty of warm layers.

New England's rocky beaches can be intimidating, but great rewards await the bold.

Prime striper locations will test an angler's resolve—often with a face full of chilly brine.

This big striper really wanted that plug!

Other Opportunities

Although treacherously rocky shores abound, New England also offers plenty of less demanding striper spots.

"Crazy" Alberto Knie shows off this fine striper caught on a bucktail jig.

Although perilous perches, strenuous casting and the nearly obsessive pursuit of giant stripers seem synonymous with New England fishing, this region is no one-trick pony. Surf species diversity may be a little thinner than those of Southern regions, but fishing opportunities offer something for all levels of interest and ability, with options ranging from the rough and rugged to the truly tranquil. Intimidating rocky coasts are never far away, but New England lacks not for convenient, family-friendly shores like Cape Cod's expansive eastern edge, New Hampshire's Hampton Beach, or Maine's Popham, Old Orchard, Fortune Rocks and Plum Island beaches.

"It all depends on what you want to do," Jenkins said of Northeastern shoreline opportunities. "On a sandy beach, chunk-

striper fanatics—those wicked teeth really do a number on one's expensive plugs—these ravenous predators offer sport aplenty. For starters, intense feeding competition means the schooling blues rarely turn down a potential meal, so fire off pretty much any of those worn-out, soon-to-be-replaced striper plugs and it's game on. Bucktails, spoons, diamond jigs (aka "tins") and anything that looks like a fleeing baitfish will also end up with teeth marks.

The year's last quarter sees false albacore adding another target to the mix. Knie said he finds the albacore timid at the front end of their arrival, but after a couple of weeks they'll acclimate themselves to the area's habitat and crank up the feeding aggression. Anglers targeting false albacore use flies and a mixed bag of artificials to nab these speedy sport fish.

ing can be more of a relaxed style of fishing where you're throwing out chunks of bait and waiting for something to happen. Striped bass are the primary target and most of their feeding is at night, so if you want to have an easy night, take a beach chair and a rod holder and throw chunks on a beach. If you want to be a little more aggressive, you put your waders and Korkers on, find a good rock to stand on and you throw your plugs into the darkness."

Another casual endeavor: freelining live eels on low, sandy beaches. Jenkins said the pre-made lead and hook rigs available at most local tackle shops are fine for rigging eels through the lips (bottom to top), making short lobs and steadily retrieving just fast enough to keep baits off the bottom. Plastic eels on jigheads also work and most strikes, Jenkins said, come within 20 feet of the beach.

Despite the snubbing bluefish receive from

"In the early season, they're extremely finicky, but as the season progresses, particularly in September, they just go crazy," Knie said. "You can catch them on tins. You can catch them on swimmers. You can even catch them on poppers and rubber shads."

New England surf fishing also offers summer flounder (fluke), found over mudflats with nearby eelgrass, jetties, shell beds and wharf pilings. Light fishfinder rigs baited with sand worms, blood worms or pieces of clam or mussel will tempt the flatties. Tautog, although generally considered an offshore species, also follow the tides to inshore feeding grounds. Look for 'togs around rocky shorelines, pilings, jetties and shellbeds and freeline pieces of worms or crabs (green, rock, hermit or fiddler).

Complementing New England's stellar striper action, bluefish, false albacore and flounder offer diversity.

Bait & Tackle Shops

Kittery Trading Post
301 U.S. Route One
Kittery, ME 03904
(888) 587-6246

Canal Bait and Tackle
101 Cranberry Hwy
Sagamore, MA 02561
(508) 833-2996

Hull Bait & Tackle
288 Atlantic Ave.
Hull, MA 02045
(781) 925-4667

Ocean State Tackle
430 Branch Ave.
Providence, R.I. 02904
(401) 226-6626

Saco Bay Tackle Company
977 Portland Rd, US1
Saco, ME 04072
(207) 284-4453

Piers & Jetties

Pemberton Point Pier
183 Main Street
Hull, MA 02045
781-925-0239

Accessible jetties are at:
- Rhode Island's Weekapaug, Quonochontaug and Charlestown breachways along with the long west jetty and the eastern breakwater at Point Judith

- Cape Cod's Harwich Port (east end of Merkel Beach)

- Scussets Beach, Mass. (north side of Cape Cod Canal)

- Maine's Wells Harbor jetties (both sides)

Magnificent natural scenery, rich angling history and incredible fishing action define the New England surf appeal.

Along with its notorious rocky shorelines, New England also holds many flat beaches with solid fishing potential.

Bright Ideas

With nocturnal feeding preferences, striped bass typically bring their best game after dark. Experienced anglers will hit the beach or take to the rocks rigged and ready, but snags, break-offs and bluefish happen, so re-rigging is just part of the deal. Organization, which starts with prudent tackle selection (read: keep it simple), minimizes time-killing searches, but even with a full moon illuminating objects below, you'll want to make sure you can see into a gear bag or tackle tray or scan the sand/rocks for the occasional dropped item.

Keeping your gear and tackle boxes organized helps you easily locate items at night.

Keep a waterproof flashlight handy and secure it in a zippered pocket, or on a flexible lanyard clipped to your wading belt. Other options include clip-on hat lights and mini flashlights worn on neck lanyards or clipped to a tackle pack handle with a D-ring. For stationary fishing (i.e. beach chairs and rod holders), a press-on dome light (home supply stores) offer a soft flood light effect for the shoreline. Not only will this provide light for rigging needs, but it also provides a distance reference should you or anyone in your group hike down the beach to scout other opportunities.

Another nocturnal consideration is tackle availability. Not all bait and tackle shops remain open during peak nighttime striper hours, so make sure you have all the lures and terminal tackle you need, with backups for all. There's not much worse than losing a key bait or running out of that hook size or swivel you need at the peak of a hot bite. Some shops in fishing communities keep vending machines with everything from natural baits to terminal tackle outside and accessible 24/7. You might find a fellow angler with spare tackle, but don't expect any bargains on the beach.

A shovel will work, but a pitch fork is best as it cuts through hard sand but doesn't split your worms in half.

Sand worms are a great bait for stripers, but watch out for their pinchers or you could be in for a painful surprise.

Hook multiple sand worms and let them free float in the current. The dangling ends will entice strikes.

Striper Fishing Maine Estuaries

Experiencing a morning sunrise and knowing [so]me quality striper fishing is ahead of you makes [w]aking up at the crack of dawn well worth it for [an]y fisherman. Our destination is Saco, Maine, [w]here my father and I take a few trips per year to [eith]er surf or kayak fish for the schools of linesid[er]s. Here, the tide rises and falls twice per day, so [pl]anning out your trip and fishing locations is cru[cia]l to having a successful day on the water. Pick [up] a current tide chart at a local bait shop and ask [th]em what bait to use, method, and where to use it

have to dig in a few different areas before you finally run into them, in which you should also find clams and mussels in the same hole as well. Be careful when you do find some sand worms, because they will emit a set of pinchers from their head that may give an unwanted early morning wakeup call.

Digging your own sand worms yields ultimate striper candy.

Once you find some decent size worms, a 2/0 hook with a 1-ounce pyramid sinker will get you down in the surf where there isn't much current, possibly adding some fluorescent beads free sliding on the line to add color and attractant. Use heavier weight if fishing near an estuary where the tide is ripping. We like to run the worm up the hook and also loop it a few times to give it some mass when floating around and make it more appealing for a striper swimming by. When fishing from a kayak and floating with the tide, a small split shot may be used or just free floating a hook full of sandworms will slowly sink into strike zone.

At any rate, fishing with sandworms provides a relaxing environment where your kids can hunt for worms; a hungry striper will gladly serve himself lunch and will also keep your wallet a bit more happy. Give it a try when you are in the area!
—*Mark Naumovitz*

School sized stripers are fun to catch and offer non-stop action.

[to] increase your chances of bending a rod. The preferred bait we would use to surf fish and [dri]ft with our kayaks would be sand worms. You [ca]n purchase them at the bait shop or you can dig [for] them like we would, giving you the most fresh [an]d usually sizeable worms that you can instantly [pu]t on a hook. Some type of shovel to get you down [is n]eeded but we would prefer to use a stiff type of [pit]ch fork, which would allow you to get through the [gro]und without much effort, and would also prevent [yo]u from cutting your worms in half.

[ ]Most of the worms are about eight to twelve [in]ches down in the earth, and in an area where moist [bu]t firm sand will mix with nutrient rich mud. You may

Sunset striper fishing. A bell is affixed to a rod tip to signal a fish bite.

CHAPTER 10

Mid-Atlantic

One of the most diverse regions on the Eastern Seaboard, the Mid-Atlantic blends the seaside splendor of Virginia Beach with the remoteness of barrier island beaches along the Delmarva Peninsula, adds in a mosaic of sights and sounds from the Jersey Shore and concludes with the legendary ruggedness of Long Island's Montauk Point. Truly a mix of casual and hardcore, this region keeps the surf scene rocking with something for all angling interests.

Between the Outer Banks and New England, the Mid-Atlantic offers one of the East Coast's most diverse regions.

At the upper end of the region, casting from rocky pedestals (above) often delivers big fish (right).

Mid-Atlantic Magic

Throughout the Mid-Atlantic, a cozy, seaside vibe is seldom far away.

For simplicity, we'll divide the Mid-Atlantic region into three main sections, New York and the Jersey Shore (upper end), the Delmarva Peninsula shared by Delaware, Maryland, Virginia (central) and the Virginia Beach strip at the south side of Chesapeake Bay. In the lower end, Virginia's southeastern corner carries over the same tactics and species mix of North Carolina's Outer Banks. From False Cape State Park, across Rudee Inlet to Virginia Beach with its namesake pier and northward to Cape Henry, spring through fall finds a good selection of trout, croakers, whit-ing, spot, flounder and bluefish in the surf.

Spring sees a big run of giant red drum heading toward Chesapeake Bay and fall brings round two, as the reds exit the bay to feed along the shallow surf before heading to their offshore spawning grounds. Heavy-action 10- to 12-foot surf outfits and fishfinder rigs baited with cut mullet or menhaden are the usual offerings for big bull reds, with smaller drum often taken closer to the beach on lighter tackle.

Pier anglers find a live finger mullet on a Carolina rig an easy sell to any flounder settled below, while double-drop rigs baited

When the bite's on at Long Island Beach, anglers will have plenty of company.

From rugged, rocky shores to placid, sandy beaches, the Mid-Atlantic offers something for everyone.

Made to imitate baitfish like finger mullet (left), spoons cast like a dream and sport inherent action.

Toothy bluefish are one of the most aggressive species you'll find in the Mid-Atlantic surf.

Pick your habitat and surf preference—Mid-Atlantic waters deliver diversity.

with shrimp, clam or small chunks of mullet or menhaden appeal to trout, spot, croakers, whiting and black drum. Shark anglers tie into blacktips, bulls, sand sharks and the occasional thresher with heavy tackle and steel leader rigs baited with large chunks of mackerel, mullet or bluefish, while live menhaden or mullet on wire rigs will tap into the summer kingfish bite.

At the region's other end, striped bass pursuits attract passionate attention throughout coastal New Jersey and New York. For hardcore striped bass surf casting, few areas rival the east end of New York's Long Island, particularly Montauk Point and Orient Point, along with their adjacent Block and Plum islands, respectively. Long Island summers see a large tourism crowd, but

fall belongs to serious surf fishermen who often negotiate slick, rocky footing that would make a mountain goat nervous. This scene is not particularly kind to novices and with powerful waves complicating matters, you really need to know what you're doing, or buddy up with someone who does. This area is one of the most famous surf fishing spots in the country, along with North Carolina's Outer Banks; Hilton Head Island, South Carolina; New Smyrna, Florida; Padre Island, Texas.

Clusters of boats nudging as close as possible to Montauk's coast and the unforgiving shallows indicate the presence of stripers. During the height of the action, veteran anglers will show up early to claim a good position in the "picket fence" of anglers lined up nearly shoulder-to-shoulder.

From Sandy Hook to Cape May (site of a landmark WWII bunker), beautiful open beaches stretch across a collection of barrier islands and on through the mainland shores. Except for a few isolated islets, bridges linking the Jersey Shore beaches to the mainland and to one another provide direct access to a wide range of surf fishing spots (The Cape May-Lewes Ferry provides a direct link from the Delmarva Peninsula, west of Cape Henlopen, to the Jersey Shore.)

Waves of Fun

From Virginia Beach to the Montauk Point, the Mid-Atlantic has a deep history of surf fishing.

With the sun behind him, this angler has a clear view of the surf action.

Long stretches of desolate beaches allow Delmarva anglers to space out and find their fish.

Jersey's serious striper anglers prefer the night action and tempt their fish with a mix of poppers, darters, swimbaits and bucktails. Lacking much pronounced rocky structure, Jersey anglers pick their beaches carefully, based on wind direction and bait concentrations. Numerous breakwaters spiking the Jersey Shore provide helpful structure, as do the jetties at Cape May Inlet, Great Egg Harbor Inlet (north side) and Barnegat Inlet (both sides).

For the casual angler, soaking chunks of bunker off sandy beaches like Belmar, Point Pleasant and most anywhere along the upper Sandy Hook peninsula, or free-lining live eels in the surf or at the jetties will deliver plenty of striper action. Adding to the fun, bluefish love those spoons, bucktails and Gotcha Plugs, but they'll also pick up cut baits fished on high-low (double dropper) rigs.

The Delmarva Peninsula offers great stretches of pristine beaches spread mostly across narrow barrier islands separated from the mainland by salt marshes and inner islands. From Smith Island north through the Metompkin Islands, the southern half of these ocean beaches lay detached from the peninsular mainland. Anglers in private boats or kayaks can easily reach the western shores, where a reasonable walk grants access to the Atlantic beaches.

Mainland access begins at Wallops Island, home to NASA's Mid-Atlantic Regional Space Center, where limited recreational access is allowed south of the center's boundary. To the north, Virginia and Maryland split the 37-mile-long Assateague Island, parts of which include its namesake National Seashore, Assateague State Park and the Chincoteague National Wildlife Refuge. The only mainland connection runs through Chincoteague Island at the south end, but the park allows a limited number of permitted off-road vehicles. Otherwise, hiking to distant spots, or reaching northern points by private vessel are your options.

Across Ocean City Inlet, Fenwick is the last barrier island before peninsular mainland starts on the north side of Indian River Inlet and continues through Cape Henlopen. Fenwick holds the more tourism-centered beaches like the popular Ocean City strip, but this entire stretch of sand all the way to the cape holds superb surf fishing waters. Just consider that heavier beach crowds will limit your line placements and position your rods prudently.

Mid-Atlantic surf anglers who spend a bit of time on the beach sometimes proudly mark their spots with makeshift structures.

On the long, shallow beaches of Assateague Island, the scent of live bait helps to attract fish.

Shallow Surf, Deep Opportunity

Some Mid-Atlantic beaches allow permitted off-road vehicles, but always check local regulations.

Favoring the tranquility of Assateague's more lightly travelled shores, Maryland angler Rob Dunning said that the entire Delmarva coast sees a very gradual bottom declination that leaves a wide band of shallow water bordering the coast. It's not uncommon, he said, to see surfers 300 yards from shore waiting on the next wave while standing in only chest-deep water. Nevertheless, Assateague's assortment of striped bass, red drum, trout, flounder, croakers, black drum and bluefish represents the Delmarva bounty. The area's abundance befits its natural splendor—you have to work with what the region offers.

"Because of the shallow depths, our water tends to be a little more off-colored, from the sand being stirred up in the water," Dunning said.

Given this silty scenario, Dunning said that plug casting much of the Delmarva coast re-

quires a lot of walking to probe the waters in hopes of locating aggressive fish. Natural baits, he said, are far more effective, as the benefits of scent and multiple offerings helps an angler cover more water and draw surf species into the fishing area. Noting that his tactics apply to most any Mid-Atlantic beach, Dunning said that natural baiting may, at times, also require a mobile mindset.

"If things are kind of slow, I'll leap-frog to cover more beach," he said. "I might start at Point A and work south to Point B and Point C. I may fish four or five rods and with every bait change, I'll reel in my northernmost rod, change the bait, go down below my southernmost rod, cast it out and work the beach that way."

With broad, flat beaches that are lean on discernible features, it's important to pay close attention to the dynamics of wave height and run-

Mid-Atlantic surf anglers find vast opportunity, even in meager depths.

Mid-Atlantic surf anglers find vast opportunity, even in meager depths.

The Mid-Atlantic offers plenty of adventurous angling to balance the casual stuff.

Clouds of birds flying close to the surface are a sure sign of feeding fish.

outs, while looking for any beach points, depth variances and fresh crustacean shells that indicate recent feeding. Throughout the fishing season, and certainly from year to year, he notes, Atlantic storms will alter the landscape. Therefore, treating each trip like a new scouting mission is the right approach.

Dunning, who plans most of his trips around the spring and fall striped bass migrations, said these fish will feed very close to shore, especially at night, but long casts to distant fish are the norm. Clam or bunker chunks on fish finders with durable nylon sinker slides slipped onto braided main line tied directly to the hook are common. This setup allows stripers and other fish to pick up your bait and run, with the circle hook setting before the fish feels any sinker resistance.

On open beaches with virtually no obstructions, Dunning appreciates the stretch and low cost of monofilament, so he uses an inverted version of this fish rig. Starting with a 2-foot leader of 100-pound monofilament, he ties a barrel swivel at the top end, which links to his main line snap. He ties the leader's other end to a Duo-Lock snap that holds his 4- to 8-ounce sinker. Before attaching the Duo-Lock, he'll run his leader through one ring of a barrel swivel with a 6-inch, 50-pound monofilament leader holding an 8/0 snelled circle hook tied to the other ring.

"The fish can't run (as far) as with some of these other rigs without feeling the weight, but there's still enough play," Dunning said. "When I cast, the weight's at the bottom and the bait's hanging off to the side, so I don't have much helicoptering. Also, when I used to rig with the hook on the bottom and the weight sliding above it, you'd have a pinch point on the leader where the sinker pulls right above the hook. It puts a kink in the leader because of the force (from) casting and it would wear down the leader. With the way I rig now, that doesn't happen. But if the hook or its leader needs replacing, I just cut it off at the barrel where it slides on the main leader and retie."

Even those with a strong preference for natural baits will want to keep a good selection of artificials handy for targets of opportunity and the occasional blitz where stripers and/or bluefish ravage baitfish close to shore. A good selection will include swim shads, large Gotcha Plugs, spoons and Crippled Herring for daytime casting and

Even with a solid natural bait setup, you'll want to keep a few artificials ready for targeted casting.

Striped bass are the top target along much of the Mid-Atlantic coast.

Small bluefish are one of the many species available in the Mid-Atlantic surf.

Super aggressive blues will readily attack large surf plugs.

poppers and swimbaits for after dark.

Rubber eels on ½-ounce jigheads also tempt stripers, as well as the cobia that occasionally wander into the surf zone. And don't forget the white bucktail with a soft-plastic tail. The anytime-utility player for surf anglers anywhere, the bucktail tempts Mid-Atlantic stripers, bluefish and weakfish when ripped through the waves, while flounder like it hopped or dragged along the bottom.

Among the other Del-marva surf targets, seatrout (aka "gray" trout), flounder, smaller black and red drum and whiting are commonly taken on high-low rigs baited with clam, shrimp or blood worms and sweetened with pieces of Fishbites (scent enhancement strips). On the larger end of the spectrum, the Mid-Atlantic surf sees a lot of shark activity, as these savvy predators leverage the expansive shallows to run down their prey.

Ben Dziwulski has spent many summers pulling bull,

Bait & Tackle Shops

Paulie's Tackle of Montauk
S. Edgemere St.
Montauk, NY 11954
(631) 668-5520

Cape May Bait and Tackle
719 Broadway
West Cape May, NJ 08204-4155
(609) 898-6001

Barnegat Light Bait & Tackle
1501 Bayview Ave
Sayreville, NJ 08006
(609) 494-4566

Captain Steve's Bait & Tackle
6527 Maddox Blvd.
Chincoteague Island, VA 23336
(757) 336-0569

Oceanside Bait & Tackle
8201 Long Beach Blvd
Brighton Beach, NJ 08008
(609) 361-9800

Long Bay Pointe Bait & Tackle
2109 West Great Neck Road
Virginia Beach, VA 23451
(757) 481-7517

Piers & Jetties

Steeplechase Park Pier
(Coney Island Public Beach)
Surf Ave. Between W. 16 St. and W. 19 St.
Brooklyn, NY 11224

Virginia Beach Pier
1506 Atlantic Ave
Virginia Beach, VA 23451
(757) 428-2333

Cape Henlopen State Park Pier
15099 Cape Henlopen Drive
Lewes, DE 19958
(302) 645-8983

Ocean City Pier
401 South Atlantic Ave.
Ocean City, MD 21842
(410) 289-3031

tiger, sandbar, sand tiger, dusky, blacktip, spinner, thresher, Atlantic sharpnose and lemon sharks onto the sands. He gears up with heavy boat tackle in the 50- to 130-pound range (Penn Senator 6/0 or bigger) and fishes fresh, bloody baits like tuna carcasses or chunks of stingray, skate, bluefish or mahi-mahi. Dziwulski uses a sit-on-top kayak to paddle the bait out 150 to 300 yards or more, drops the rig and returns to shore where one of his beach teammates has secured the rod in a holder made from sturdy galvanized pipe.

Dziwulski said it's important to have at least one person watching the line during bait deployment to prevent tangles. Once the bait is set, reel up the slack until the rod tip bends slightly. Setting the drag at about 3 to 5 pounds with the reel clicker engaged, allows a shark to pick up the bait and swim off without detecting any pressure. Once the fight is underway, a multi-person team will need to assist the angler with stability, beaching, dehooking and reviving/releasing the shark as quickly as possible.

"Shark fishing is extremely dangerous and is not for inexperienced fishermen," Dziwulski said. "Never shark fish with less than 4 people on hand, as you must be prepared for anything. Always wear a life jacket while kayaking, and be prepared for emergencies. It is a dangerous sport, but when done properly with an experienced crew, it is a thrilling experience!"

Accessible jetties are at:
- Inlets between the barrier islands flanking New York's Long Island (ex. Jones Island)

- Breezy Point at Long Island's southern tip

- Indian River Inlet (north end of Fenwick Island)

- Manasquan Inlet (Jersey Shore)

- Ocean City Inlet south jetty (north end of Assateague Island).

Don't Be Selfish With a Shellfish

Hard-charging black drum have a taste for fresh clams.

It's a Mid-Atlantic tradition: stomping across low-tide mud flats and dragging "clam rakes" to dislodge and scoop up the tasty mollusks. Wading in tidal shallows and feeling around with your feet, or looking for the telltale signs of a buried clam offer less strenuous options, but the common objective remains the same. A lot of recreationally harvested clams end up in the

Freshly-shucked clams yield a tasty bait that appeals to a variety of surf species.

steamer, but some gatherers have bigger plans in mind—specifically, a day of surf fishing.

Indeed, a fresh clam makes one mean surf bait for striped bass, bluefish, black drum, redfish and just about anything else swimming the bars and troughs. Shucking these succulent shellfish for bait takes the same care you'd invest for those destined for the steamer. Essentially, make sure you carefully sever the muscles connecting the animal to its shell so you end up removing the entire body, especially the tasty belly section and the smelly entrails, which help the fish locate your bait.

If you lack the time and/or interest for collecting your own fresh clams, local seafood wholesalers can provide the next best thing. Frozen clam strips sold at bait shops will also work, but make sure they're brined for durability.

Clams in any stage of freshness require rigging diligence, with a threading pattern—multiple loops on the hook—your best bet. (Smaller pieces of clam strip are less tedious.) Even when properly hooked, all that soft flesh tends to wriggle and wiggle with the slightest movement. The energy of a long cast can rip the hook from your clam bait and send it flying off. Avoid this by securing the bait with a few wraps of Ghost Cocoon Thread— a monofilament that cinches on itself and holds the clam in place. (Check your state's regulations for clam size and bag limit before harvesting. Season and area closures may also apply.)

Go generous with your clam bait and thread the bait onto the hook.

Walking muddy beaches with a clam rake delivers your choice of shellfish dinner or excellent Mid-Atlantic bait.

CHAPTER 11

North Carolina

North Carolina's feature-rich coast combines three major hooks— (south to north) Cape Fear, Cape Lookout and Cape Hatteras—with the renowned Outer Banks, and this terrain presents a lot of fishable stretches. Some areas offer straightforward access, others require a little more effort in the approach, but surf fishing is generally pretty convenient in the Tar Heel State.

A barber pole de distinguishes N Carolina's Cape teras Lighthous

Long stretches of open beach, often guarded by grassy sand dunes and bordered by a fertile Atlantic surf—that's the North Carolina coast.

Carolina Calls

A trio of capes and a lengthy chain of barrier islands give North Carolina tremendous coastal character.

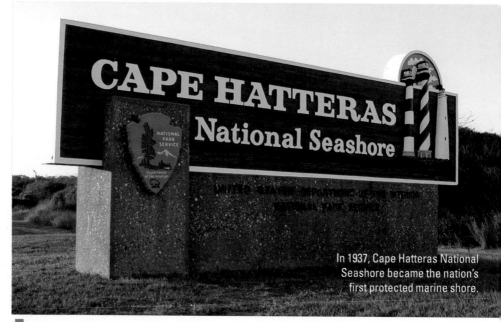

In 1937, Cape Hatteras National Seashore became the nation's first protected marine shore.

ocally known as the OBX, the state's dominant northern barrier islands may be little more than glorified sand bars in geological terms, but reaching approximately 130 miles from North Carolina's upper boundary to Ocracoke Island about mid-state, they guard the massive Albemarle and Pamlico sounds—among the world's largest estuaries. Moreover, Cape Hatteras National Seashore (est. 1937), which extends more than 70 miles from South Nags Head to Ocracoke Inlet, was the nation's first effort to protect marine shores.

With the coast taking a semi-crescent shape from cape to cape (and Cape Fear to Georgetown, S.C), you'll find the nearshore currents varying from a straight east-west approach to more of a lateral course inside each "hook." Consistent for the region is the bountiful intersection of the cold northern Labrador Current and the warmer Gulf Stream. The resulting integration just north of the OBX creates some of the world's most fertile fishing grounds—a benefit extending well into the surf zone.

Anglers can look for more northern-oriented species such as bluefish, weakfish and striped bass, along with the speckled trout, flounder, mackerel, croakers, whiting and spot that range more southward. From about Cape Lookout through the OBX, oversized red drum (aka "bull reds") are the rock stars of the surf scene. Smaller slot-sized "puppy" drum roam the entire coast, as well as the inlets and sounds throughout much of the year, but spring and fall finds copper brutes of 50-plus pounds feeding on nearshore forage on their way to and from northern spawning grounds. Big reds

In the historic village of Corolla, the Currituck Lighthouse overlooks the north end of the famed Outer Banks.

 are not unheard of below the middle cape, but with the coastline sloping away from the deep water, the major push of bull reds tends to bypass the shallower, low-impact beaches of Onslow Bay and Long Bay, where a nice assortment of smaller surf species picks up the slack.

Joe Malat, former OBX surf guide and Director of the Outer Banks Surf Fishing School, penned his own book on surf tactics. He notes that while piers and inlets present stationary spots of concentrated activity, the breaks in coastal bars create current-funneling centers

North Carolina surf fishing hot spots like Atlantic Beach, left, yield a variety of species, including bluefish, right.

of activity along open beaches throughout the OBX and down through the lower coast. Worth noting, the U.S. Life Saving Service—predecessor of the U.S. Coast Guard—began building life-saving stations along the Carolina coast in the late 1800s to rescue crews frequently stranded on treacherous shoals and reefs. The first of seven stations was named Chicamacomico— Algonquian for "Land of Sinking Sand" and a pretty good summary of the region's dynamics.

"Good surf fishing locations can pop up almost anywhere, depending on how the winds and currents have formed the beach and created those outer bars, sloughs and breaks in the bars," Malat said. "There's a coarser sand (with pebbles) along the northern beaches, whereas it's a finer-grain, closely-packed sand that you see frequently on the southern end of North Carolina. The coarser sand is not always indicative of a better place to fish, but it indicates a more dynamic coastal process."

Anglers looking to lock horns with one of those behemoth red drum will appreciate how that dynamic coastal process creates the feeding opportunities sufficient to satisfy some pretty big appetites. Historically, the crossing currents of Cape Point at the tip of Cape Hatteras have marked the Mecca of giant red drum action, with anglers standing nearly shoulder-to-shoulder, awaiting the next round of absolute mayhem when a pod of big drum swings down the beach. Nighttime is typically most active, as the big fish are mostly nocturnal feeders.

"I believe Cape Point is the best place in the world to surf fish," Malat said. "You have a really

North Carolina owes its incredibly fertile waters to the intersection of the cold Labrador Current and the warmer Gulf Stream.

good chance of catching a really big red drum. You can see on a map how that spot sticks out into the ocean. You have the currents that run north to south and when the wind shifts and currents come from the south, they meet head-on. And then you have the Diamond Shoals—that shallow water that runs several miles out into the ocean—that's just a constantly upturned buffet line that holds big red drum."

(Note: In the interest of shorebird and sea turtle nesting habitat, the National Park Service

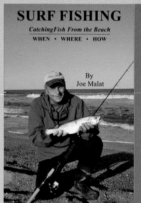

Longtime North Carolina angler Joe Malat authored his own surf fishing book that includes lots of helpful tips on baits, rigging, etc.

imits access to certain areas of Cape Hatteras National Seashore and restricts access to others, so check with local tackle shops, the North Carolina Beach Buggy Association or the NPS for current regulations.)

Malat, the former Director of the North Carolina Aquarium, pegs the boundaries of predictable big red action at Oregon Inlet (between Bodie Island and Pea Island) and Cape Lookout. Malat said he's found the beaches of Rodanthe, Avon and Buxton especially productive, thanks to their pronounced bars and deep sloughs. Prime months are May, October and November, with fall bringing the best action.

"Water temperature drives everything," Malat said. "In the spring, the Atlantic water takes forever to get warm. It's a 1- or 2-degree change over a several week period. You have that window in late-April through May when those fish are coming in from offshore and moving into the Chesapeake Bay. In the fall, the water has been warm all summer and you get those first cold fronts that come through, the northeast wind shifts, the water temperature starts to drop and it's like a switch gets thrown. Those big fish come off the barrier islands on the eastern shore of Virginia, funnel out of Chesapeake Bay and more north-to-south along the Outer Banks. It I had to pick a really good period, it would be mid-October to mid-November."

Complementing the Virginia fish, another body of fish, which spends its summers in Pamlico River, lingers around the mouth of the Pamlico River. Once cooling weather and shortening days usher these fish out through the inlets, they'll mingle with the northern group for one voracious crimson convoy that basically chews its way down the beach before heading to offshore spawning grounds.

Fresh mullet is the top spring bait, with fresh menhaden the fall preference. Terminal tackle is decidedly uncomplicated—a fishfinder rig with 8 inches of 80- to 100-pound fluorocarbon leader tied to a 7/0-10/0 circle hook. The short leader keeps the rig from helicop-

North Carolina's Outer Banks, especially the Cape Hatteras area, are famous for producing bull redfish.

tering on the cast, and since a circle hook typically grabs the fish in the corner of its mouth, there's no need for a longer rig.

Most serious red drum anglers are heaving rigs with 8 to 10 ounces of lead on 12- to 14-foot rods that punch the baits out past the nearshore froth and into the deeper water where reds feed. Heavy sinkers require tremendous force on these long casts and that can inflict a lot of pressure and abrasion on a standard sinker slide's plastic collar. Prevent tackle failure by using sinker slides with more durable nylon collars.

On rare occasion that you see a school of big

Shifting sands and crossing currents mean that good fishing could pop up just about anywhere along North Carolina's Outer Banks.

Above and at right, smaller "puppy drum" keep anglers busy between the runs of oversized Carolina reds.

reds feeding on top, you can catch them on bucktails and poppers. That's mostly for boaters, but occasionally pier anglers get their shots at these flurries.

Complementing the arm-stretching revelry of bull red fishing, North Carolina surf anglers occasionally tangle with quality stripers. The hefty cows of Northeast fame show up less frequently here, but January-March brings plenty of fish well into the double digits. Ryan White, custom surf rod builder and owner of Hatteras Jack Bait & Tackle, spends a lot of time on state beaches and bases his striper strategy on striper density.

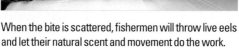

When the bite is scattered, fishermen will throw live eels and let their natural scent and movement do the work.

"If the fish are scattered, it's mostly bait fishing because bait tends to pull up the big ones," White said. "If there's a concentration

of them, we'll start using artificials."

Top natural baits are cut bunker and squid, or cracked calico crabs on fishfinder rigs with 7/0-10/0 circle hooks, 6- to 8-ounce weights and 2-inch leaders that optimize casting. The idea, White said, is to introduce maximum scent into the water so the fish find your bait. Live eels are mostly used around inlets, but they occasionally work on the beach, as well. Use a standard fishfinder rig or lip-hook the eel on a jig. (Some use eel skins as plug trailers.)

Common striped bass artificials include darters, Polaris Poppers and Crocodile or Hopkins spoons. Even when bait fishing, White said it's wise to keep an artificial rod handy for the random "blitz" of stripers or blues attacking a pod

Big stripers complement the North Carolina redfish action.

of bait close to shore. For smaller blues, just drop down a size or two in plugs and spoons.

Other large surf targets include a spring run of cobia and summer-fall tarpon migrations. Subsurface plugs like the Bomber Long A, bucktails and most live baits appeal to cobes, while fish finders with chunks of bluefish or mullet, or live baits like blue crab, mullet, or croaker tempt the tarpon.

For a mixed bag of smaller surf species some of North Carolina's more productive beaches include Corolla (upper end of OBX), North End of Pea Island (beach side and Oregon Inlet jetty), south end of Ocracoke Island (mainland ferry from Cedar Island or Swann Quarter), Cape Lookout (ferry from Harkers Island and then a long walk to the point), east end of Ocean Isle Beach facing Shallotte Inlet.

When targeting the speckled trout that congregate on the beaches each spring and fall, Malat wades with a 7- to 8-foot rod spooled with 10-pound braid and throws curly tail jigs and suspending baits like MirrOlure 52M and TT. Bumping bottom is essential, he said, so he'll cast onto the top of a bar; work the bait down through the slough and right up to the "drop" where waves carve a mini shelf against the shore. Finger mullet, silversides and other forage gather here, so expect plenty of bites super shallow.

"The red head/white body MirrOlure is an all-time classic that still works great today," said Sam White (no relation to Ryan), who grew up wading the shores of Wrightsville Beach through the OBX. "Second choice is match-the-hatch silver side with green or black back to resemble a finger mullet. For the grubs, chartreuse is a popular

Fresh mullet and menhaden are the top baits for those huge Carolina redfish.

Above, an angler faces east into a Carolina sunrise, while here, anglers enjoy a sunset across Cape Hatteras.

color along with a silver flake, both with red lead head jigs. The MirrOlures produce fewer bites but bigger fish, while the grubs would always find a way to get bit by something—drum, flounder, trout, or some surprise fish.

"Bucktails also work well. You can sling 'em a mile and either bounce the bottom for flounder, trout or drum or rip them across the top for bluefish. I like white or yellow with the opposite color curly tail. Spoons are good too, and the original Hopkins really made a name for itself on the big bluefish off the Outer Banks. Same deal, you can cast it a mile for bluefish and Spanish mackerel."

Croakers, whiting, spot, puppy drum and black drum offer plenty of casual fare from most any Carolina beach. Most are taken with shrimp or cut bait (mullet or menhaden) on 2-drop bottom rigs (available in most tackle shops) or Fireball Rigs (a version of the double dropper with fluorescent Stryofoam floats above the hooks to keep baits higher in the water).

For flounder, on the beach or near jetties and piers, fish live or dead finger mullet or a strip of mullet on a ¼-ounce leadhead. Fan cast to

From the inside edge of Cape Hatteras, an angler casts into the setting sun.

For stripers in the Carolina surf, anglers throw artificials (left) when the fish are concentrated.

locate the fish and retrieve your bait in sweeps. You'll do best on calmer days when less current allows you to better manage your presentations. False albacore, known locally as "Fat Alberts," give surf casters a reel-screaming thrill when marauding schools swing in close to hotspots like "The Hook" (northwest corner) of Cape Lookout. Clousers and deceivers on 10-weight fly rods, spoons, jigs and even topwater plugs will find a taker.

At the jetties, plugs with treble hooks tend to find trouble around rocks and their accumulated clutter. Your best bet here is bouncing leadhead grub jigs or bucktails. Single hooks snag less frequently and you can work the water column from top to bottom. Another option: Mimic the crustaceans living amid jetty rocks with D.O.A. Shrimp or Berkley Gulp! Crabs and Shrimp fished on leadheads.

Here and above, North Carolina anglers enjoy plenty of striper action with natural bait or artificial plugs.

Bait & Tackle Shops

TW's Bait & Tackle
2230 S Croatan Highway
Nags Head, NC 27959
(252) 441-4807

Hatteras Jack
23902 Highway 12
Rodanthe, NC 27968
(252) 987-2428

Red Drum Tackle
Highway 12 PO Box 1354
Buxton, NC 27920
(252) 995-5414

Capt. Joe's Bait & Tackle
601-H Atlantic Beach CSWY
Atlantic Beach, NC 28512
(252) 222-0670

Ocean Isle Fishing Center
65 Causeway Dr.
Ocean Isle Beach, NC 28469
(910) 575-FISH

Piers & Jetties

Jennette's Fishing Pier
Mile Post 16 1/2 Oceanside
Nags Head, NC 27959
(252) 441-6421

Avon Fishing Pier
Highway 12
Avon, NC 27915
(252) 995-5480

Johnnie Mercer's Pier
23 E Salisbury St
Wrightsville Beach, NC 28480
910-256-4469

Oak Island (Yaupon) Fishing Pier
705 Ocean Dr
Oak Island, NC 28465
(910) 278-6464

Sunset Beach Fishing Pier
101 W. Main ST.
Sunset Beach, NC 28468
(910) 579-6630

Low light periods present great opportunities to fool a surf fish with artificials.

Accessible jetties are at:

- Oregon Inlet (south side)
- Hatteras Light (east of original lighthouse location)
- North side of Masonboro Inlet (south end of Wrightsville Beach)
- West side of Beaufort Inlet (east end of Atlantic Beach, below Fort Macon)
- East side of Little River Inlet (south end of Bird Island)

Stewards of the Sand

Formed in 1964 by off-road enthusiasts concerned about possible loss of access to Outer Banks beaches, the North Carolina Beach Buggy Association has developed into a multi-dimensional organization that promotes and advocates for off-road vehicle (ORV) access to the OBX beaches and stresses responsible stewardship of the beaches.

Viewing access to Cape Hatteras National Seashore Recreational Area as a privilege, rather than a right, the NCBBA established a partnership with the National Park Service at Cape Hatteras to assist with park protection, as well as advocate for access issues. Through-out the years, the NCBBA has initiated several programs to help enhance the park, including Operation Beach Respect (OBR)—a program jointly developed with the NPS to keep beaches clean and conserve the resource.

The NCBBA's Code of Ethics presents a 12-point outline detailing the dos and don'ts of responsible beach use—wisdom applicable for beach use everywhere. The group also provides graphs detailing current restrictions on beach access to Cape Hatteras National Seashore Recreation Area with color-coded diagrams showing where pedestrian traffic and ORVs are allowed and which areas are closed. For information, visit ncbaaonline.com.

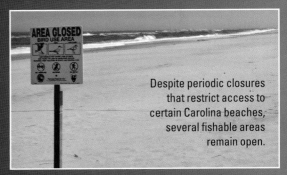

Despite periodic closures that restrict access to certain Carolina beaches, several fishable areas remain open.

From marauding bluefish, to bottom feeders like flounder, whiting, croakers and black drum, Carolina beaches present a broad range of options.

National Park Service
U.S. Department of the Interior

Cape Hatteras National Seashore

RAMP
43

Driving Information

All traffic rules apply and are enforced.

- May 1 – Sept 15
  Vehicles prohibited on beach, 10 pm – 6 am.
- Sept 16 – Nov 15
  Beach driving permit required, 10 pm – 6 am.
- All vehicles must be legal for highway use.
- 4-wheel drive vehicles recommended.
- Beach may be impassable at high tide.
- May 15–September 15
  Speed limit is 15 mph unless otherwise posted.
- September 16 – May 14
  Speed limit is 25 mph unless otherwise posted.
- Lower tire pressure to 20 PSI or less prior to entering beach.
- Pedestrians have the right of way.

Beach Regulations

Observe all posted safety and wildlife protection closures.

- Driving on dunes and vegetation is prohibited. Drive only on marked ORV routes.
- Pets must be on a six-foot leash at all times.
- Small beach fires are permitted below the high tideline and 100 feet from all vegetation. Extinguish all fires using water. No fires from 12 Midnight — 6 a.m.
- All fireworks prohibited.
- No open containers of alcoholic beverages inside motor vehicles, including pick-up truck beds. Liquor and fortified wine prohibited.
- No camping on the beach.

Violators are subject up to $5,000 fine or imprisonment of up to 6 months.
In case of emergency, dial 911.
To report a violation, dial 252-473-3444.

CHAPTER 12

South Carolina & Georgia

If you like fishing from vacation locations with a congenial mix of tourists and locals, South Carolina's Grand Strand at the north end and Hilton Head Island to the south blends beach fun with dependable rod-bending action. In between, and southward into Georgia, surf anglers find smatterings of marsh-bordered barrier islands with varying degrees of accessibility. Pick your spot, set your sand spikes and enjoy the southern charm of this pleasantly relaxed region.

Small puppy drum lead the surf catch menu throughout South Carolina and Georgia.

Beaches, barrier islands and down home Southern charm invite surf anglers to sample the local fare.

A popular summer species, Spanish mackerel like shiny, fast-moving artificials.

By the Beach

The region's lineup of surf species ranges from trout and red drum to sharks and tarpon.

The cool season may require waders and warm clothing, but good fishing lasts all year.

Spoons and other shiny lures imitate the glass minnows bluefish often chase.

Beginning with a classic "beach" look, this accessible region quickly transitions into one of fragmented coastline largely composed of thin barrier islands separated from the mainland by broad belts of spartina grass salt marshes. South Carolina's coast covers the lower two thirds of the Long Bay region that starts at North Carolina's Cape Fear. Here, the Palmetto State's upper edge comprises a blend of barrier islands and mainland beaches known as the "Grand Strand," which extends from Little River south to Georgetown. Here, you'll find long stretches of low impact beaches and relatively small inlets (compared to those farther south), along with several fishing piers.

Spring - Speckled seatrout, red drum, black drum, flounder and whiting

Summer - Red drum, seatrout, black drum, flounder, sharks, tarpon, whiting, pompano, bluefish, Spanish mackerel

Fall - Red drum, seatrout, black drum, whiting, flounder, pompano, bluefish

Winter - Red drum and whiting

From the sand or piers, anglers can expect these seasonal selections:

Productive artificials include gold or silver spoons, bucktails, leadheads with shad or curl tails and Gulp! shrimp. Those who prefer natural bait do well with shrimp, cut mullet or crab chunks on fish finder or double dropper rigs. Fiddler crabs scavenging the tidal flats commonly accessible from the mainland or barrier islands make excellent baits for sheepshead and black drum around pier pilings and jetty rocks.

When summer finds king mackerel chasing menhaden on the beach, ballooning a live bait on a wire rig will often reach far enough to entice a big bite. Same goes for tarpon and big sharks.

Along the beach, look for the usual indications of active surf and take note of the various swashes cutting through the beach and forming fish-friendly current dynamics. Among them, the Withers Swash empties out south of the 2nd Avenue Pier

Warmer months find several species of smaller sharks roaming the shallow surf.

on Myrtle Beach, while a lesser swash exits north of Springmaid Pier (Myrtle Beach), with another just north of the Sunset Beach Pier.

Most of South Carolina's barrier islands south of Georgetown are accessible only by boat until the mainland connection resumes around the Charleston Harbor Inlet area with good surf fishing opportunities on Isle of Palms, Sullivan's Island and Folly Island (nice pier on Folly). Continuing southward, surf anglers will find good access and opportunity at Edisto Island on the north side of the Saint Helena Shoal, along with Hunting and Fripp Islands to the south. The last major island with mainland access before the Georgia border is Hilton Head, where sandbars off of the north end (by Port Royal Sound) offer good spots for soaking cut mullet or menhaden on heavy fishfinder rigs for bull redfish, sharks and tarpon.

The bar system extends southeast off the island's northeast corner and with deep water reaching in between the bars and Hilton Head's southwestern shoreline slope, anglers have a wide range of depth and direction options. Depending on tide stage, the bite may be anywhere around the protruding sand bars, on the island side, the sound side, or off the southern tip toward the ocean. In addition to the heavy outfits, the warmer months will also find whiting, trout, flounder and assorted others around these bars.

The theme of surf separation continues through the Georgia coast, as Tybee Island just south of Hilton Head is one of a handful of Georgia's numerous barrier islands with mainland vehicle

Fragmented barrier islands bordered by salt marsh dominate much of the region.

access. Sapelo Island on the north side of Doboy Sound and Cumberland Island above the Florida line benefit from daily ferry service. Between them, Georgia's Golden Isles (St. Simons, Little St. Simons, Sea and Jekyll Island) link to mainland Brunswick via causeways spanning the vast Glynn County spartina fields, which inspired poet Sydney Lanier's "The Marshes of Glynn."

Georgia angler Spud Woodward said the species roundup is similar to neighboring South Carolina waters, with a few seasonal favorites. During late spring-fall, smaller Atlantic sharpnose, blacktip, spinner and bonnethead sharks are handled on medium-heavy tackle, while those who beef up to heavier conventional outfits tackle the larger lemons and bulls that hunt the surf. Slot reds are common just about year-round, but if you want bruiser bulls to the 40-pound mark, the biannual runs are April through May and then again from August through November.

You'll need big baits and heavier tackle to tempt and handle beach tarpon.

Topwaters tempt the speckled trout common through the warm season.

Carry a selection of tackle, lures and natural baits to sample the region's species mix.

Summer sees a good speckled trout bite on the Georgia beaches. Where drains cut through sandbars, expect the specks to stack up and ambush bait. Here, a topwater-and-subsurface mix of lures such as Bomber BadonkADonk topwaters, Rebel Pop-Rs, ¼-ounce jigs with 4-inch Bass Assassin paddle tails and D.O.A. Shrimp under popping floats will do the trick.

Where marsh creeks meet surf, expect flounder opportunities. Case in point: Clam Creek runs into St. Simons Sound at the north end of Jekyll and creates a popular flounder spot, while the namesake pier to the creek's west affords access to this fishery from an elevated perch that keeps you out of the mud and away from relentless marsh horse flies. Continuing around the island's north end, another marsh creek drops out at the beginning of Driftwood Beach where skeletons of hardwoods claimed by storms and polished by the sea keep surf casters company.

Spanish mackerel have been known to chase bait schools into the shallow surf, while the occasional tripletail might pass close enough for a corked shrimp presentation (if you spot him in time). Elsewhere, tarpon run the surf's deeper edges from about June to October and pompano

make scattered appearances during early fall.

Woodward's surf routine usually includes a couple of 9-foot spinning or conventional outfits with 20- to 30-pound high-visibility monofilament and a basic fishfinder rig or a modified Owen Lupton rig designed to minimize a big fish's ability to shake out even a circle hook during active feeding (see Chapter 7). Cut mullet or menhaden is his choice for sharks and bull reds, but for mid-size fish, locally-netted live finger mullet is hard to beat. For the smaller species, he scales down to 7-foot spinning outfits with 12-pound line and fishes mud minnows, killifish, cut mullet, live shrimp or Berkley Gulp! (Shrimp and Cut Bait forms) on double dropper rigs with No. 1 khale hooks or fishfinder rigs with 2- to 6-ounce weights. Currents can flow fiercely in this region, so when the water's cranking, Sputnik style weights with wire legs will keep the weight in place.

Spot, bluefish and pompano—someone had a nice day of surf fishing productivity.

Reach the Beach

Shallow-running pompano rank as one of the most prized surf species.

Given the limited coastal access along lower South Carolina and Georgia, boat fishing is the norm. However, anglers frequently take advantage of remote surf style fishing opportunities by boating to the sandbars and shoals that set up well for fishing on foot, anchoring in calm waters and taking a walk. Just about any outer bar off any barrier island can offer great surf fishing opportunities, but Capt. J.R. Waits (Fishcall.com) points to a few of his favorites:

As Capt. Greg Hildreth notes, the beauty of boat-accessed surf fishing spots is that anglers can approach from areas deeper than they typically surf fish and then fish where the water's too shallow to approach in a fishing vessel. This best-of-both-worlds scenario allows you to arrive undetected and fish largely-untouched areas.

In any of these spots, pay attention to the water level and the area in which you anchor. If your visit coincides with an outgoing tide, be sure to account for lower water so you don't return to a grounded boat. Also, when the tide falls out, if the water opposes the wind, otherwise calm sea conditions can suddenly turn treacherous.

Also note that because of its tucked-away position in the South Atlantic Bight, most Georgia beaches present perpendicular sand bars, rather than the traditional parallel bars. For example, the prominent bar behind the Jekyll Island Convention Center extends over 100 yards into the Atlantic and delivers all the usual benefits of isolated structure—bait congregation, current eddies and shallow hunting with quick access to deep water. Low tides leave a broad foot path out into the ocean, but don't let the incoming water sneak up and strand you offshore amid strong currents.

Accessible only by boat, isolated sandbars and shoals offer secluded surf fishing.

Cape Island/Lighthouse Island - (north end of Cape Romain National Wildlife Refuge)—Bull reds, sharks and tarpon.

Boneyard Beach on the upper end of Bull Island - (south end of Cape Romain National Wildlife Refuge—Bull reds, sharks, tarpon, trout, black drum, pompano and Spanish mackerel.

Deveaux Bank off of Edisto Island and Seabrook Island - (south side of North Edisto River Channel) – Bull reds, sharks, tarpon, trout, black drum and pompano.

Woodward lists some of Georgia's secluded gems:

Gould's Inlet - (between Sea Island and St. Simons) —Rocks lining the inlet are a good spot for redfish, black drum and sheepshead.

Pelican Spit - (extensive shoal/bar system at mouth of Hampton River between Sea Island and Little St. Simons Island) —Trout, whiting, flounder, redfish and sharks.

Christmas Creek - (draining a marsh between Cumberland and Little Cumberland islands) —The bars outside the creek mouth produce whiting, redfish, trout and sharks.

McQueen Inlet - (south of Middle Beach on St. Catherines Island) — Sheepshead, trout, redfish and whiting.

Big Tides Don't Wait

The biggest difference that anglers encounter when moving north to south along the South Carolina coastline is the increased tidal amplitude. The northern areas typically get 3-foot tides, whereas the southernmost areas see 8-foot tides. The pattern continues along the Georgia Coast.

Local angler Spud Woodward, who heads up the Georgia Department of Natural Resources, said that although tides vary throughout the state's coastline, the average tidal amplitude is around 6.5 feet. During astronomical high tides, he said, that range can reach over 9 feet in the central area, especially if augmented by an easterly wind. Woodward explains how Georgia's (and South Carolina's) location in the South Atlantic Bight impact local tides.

"If you think of pushing water across a floor with a squeegee and into a corner, the water level rises as it approaches the corner," Woodward notes. "We're in a corner of the Atlantic

Georgia and lower South Carolina see large tidal swings so plan accordingly.

Piers & Jetties

Cherry Grove Beach Pier
3500 N. Ocean Blvd.
North Myrtle Beach, SC 29582
(843) 249-1625

Myrtle Beach State Park Pier
4401 South Kings HWY
Myrtle Beach, SC 29575
(843) 238-5326

Surfside Pier
11 S. Ocean Blvd.
Surfside Beach, SC 29575
(843) 238-0121

Tybee Island Pier & Pavilion
Strand Ave.
Tybee Island GA 31328
(912) 652-6780

St. Simons Island Pier
121 Mallory Street
Saint Simons Island, GA 31522

Bait & Tackle Shops

Fish On Outfitters
800 Sea Mountain Hwy.
North Myrtle Beach, SC 29582
(843) 249-2600

Perry's Bait and Tackle in Murrell's Inlet
3965 Highway 17 Business
Murrells Inlet, SC 29576
(843) 651-2895

Bay Street Outfitters in Beaufort
815 Bay St.
Beaufort, SC 29902
(843) 524-5250

St. Simons Island Tackle
121 Mallory St
St Simons, GA 31522
(912) 634-1888

Jekyll Island Fishing Center shop
10 Clam Creek Road, across from campground,
Jekyll Island, GA 31527
(912) 635-3556

When a big tide turns, its course picks up tremendous momentum, so stay ahead of the water.

Ocean. As the ocean rises and falls due to the influence of the interplay of gravitational forces exerted by the earth, sun, and moon, the place in the South Atlantic Bight where this effect is most pronounced is coastal Georgia.

"Add to that the fact that the Georgia coast has a very low elevation and a very gradual change in elevation as you move from the mainland into the Atlantic Ocean. So, this twice daily rise and fall of water affects a very large area, approximately 500,000 acres of estuaries."

Such large tidal ranges mean vast low-tide drainage, which leaves broad stretches of sea bottom high and dry. Conversely, when the water returns, it's packing serious steam, so plan accordingly and know what the tide is doing before heading to the surf. Incoming tides are generally the surf fishing preference for any region, but rising water is particularly important here, as fish instinctively head for deeper water as soon as the tide turns to avoid the risk of stranding. Once this happens, locals generally pack up the surf gear because the water falls so fast and so far, the constant repositioning nets little actual fishing time.

Strong tidal movement displaces forage and stimulates predators like red drum to feed heavily.

CHAPTER 13

Florida's Atlantic Coast

Facing the Atlantic Ocean with 580 miles of mostly sandy shoreline, Florida's east coast offers the nation's largest collection of conveniently-accessed beaches. With few exceptions, such as the Kennedy Space Center security zone if you can reach it, you can fish it.

The state's upper end borrows somewhat from southern Georgia's coastal marsh look. Amelia Island, home to Florida's tallest sand dune (a 54-foot-high system named "Nana"), presents the state's first eastern land mass and sandwiches a vast spartina marsh between its west side and the Nassau County mainland. Adjacent Talbot and Little Talbot islands do likewise, with a tighter system of mainland, Intracoastal Waterway and barrier islands beginning at Jacksonville Beach, south of Mayport Inlet. From here to Miami's famed South Beach, sandy planks occasionally divided by inlets define Florida's signature Atlantic visage.

Florida's Atlantic Coast presents long strands of easily accessible beaches, several piers and fishable jetties.

Pompano and many
other species roam
Florida's picturesque
east coast beaches.

Redfish Recon

The top target along Florida's Atlantic Coast, redfish of any size fight hard in the surf.

Daytona Shores yielded a nice red for this Florida angler.

All along this eastern edge, redfish top the surf targets. Available from beach, jetty or pier, reds generally move in packs. They eat just about anything and theirs is a fight worth the effort. Jacksonville surf guru David Gill said it's easy to identify beaches with a hot redfish bite—just look for a line of anglers stacked like rods at a tackle store.

"Reds are thickest in the spring and fall, as they chase the bait (mullet) migration heading north and south," Gill said. "You can catch them year-round because they are roamers, but in the spring and fall it's almost tough not to catch them. It seems my bigger reds (over the 27-inch maximum) are in the mid-fall and most of my slot fish (18-27 inches) are in the spring run."

Reds usually feed in the outer troughs, but don't be surprised to find them chasing baitfish into the shallows of the first trench. During the prime seasons, Gill said he's always looking for a big red like his personal best 50-pounder, so it's 12-foot custom rods, big spinning reels loaded with 40-pound braid and slip sinker rigs (Carolina rig style) with 40- to 60-pound fluorocarbon leaders and 6/0 circle hooks.

"I'll vary the leader length depending on water conditions," Gill said. "Rough, confused water calls for a shorter, more controlled leader of 6 inches, while a calm day warrants a longer leader of 12 to 18 inches."

Generous chunks of freshly-caught whiting make excellent redfish bait, as do blue crabs. Gill preps a crab by clipping its claws, legs, paddles and apron (underside flap) and then splitting it

in half. One full half baits the redfish rig, while he divides the other half into "knuckles" (base of each leg joint) for smaller species. Gill said he has plenty of confidence in whiting and blue crab baits, but the hands-down favorite for big reds is a live finger mullet. This abundant coastal forage often runs in large schools, so a little surf fishing salesmanship helps close the deal.

"When the bait is thick, the key to fast hook-ups is to injure the mullet—cut off half its tail off or slice its belly," Gill said. "That makes your bait look and act differently than the 50,000 other mullet swimming in the same area.

"The reds will hit them a little more aggressively that way too. However, if you start to get hits but no commitment, that means it's time to stop injuring the baits because you're getting impulse hits instead of feeding hits."

Also In The Mix

With the exception of weakfish (prevalent in northeast Florida, but showing up more in recent years along the central coast) and the southern darlings—snook, permit and bonefish—most of the Florida surf will hold a mix of whiting, pompano, flounder, black drum, sheepshead, bluefish, Spanish mackerel and sharks. Gill said hardfighting—and tasty—pompano actually hold the top spot among hardcore surf anglers, but this is one high-strung, neurotic little fish whose gypsy ways often frustrate the casual angler.

The key, Gill notes, is monitoring the pompano migration through a network of bait shop contacts and fellow anglers. (Time on the beach and mutual assistance fuels this information engine.) With a good read on pompano positioning, Gill uses a double dropper rig with colored float beads ahead of each hook to attract attention in the surf while keeping baits off the bottom.

A pyramid sinker works in light to moderate surf, but when the water's really moving, he'll go with a Sputnik style sinker, which sprouts wire legs that dig into the sand and hold at the desired position until the angler applies line pressure to spring the wire legs into the release position. Adjusting wire tension on Sputniks, or using the more advanced missile sinkers, allows anglers to tweak the weight for various current strengths.

Homemade or store-bought, double dropper rigs will also catch whiting—probably the most popular and most commonly caught surf species among casual anglers—as well as spot, drum, sheepshead and flounder. Shrimp, brined clam strips and sand fleas are the common baits for these rigs and experienced surf anglers typically sweeten the presentation with a piece of Fishbites—a synthetic scent attractant made with a water soluble gel that disperses scent through the water.

One of Gill's favorite bait strategies is the "Clam Sandwich"—a

Ghost Cocoon Thread holds shrimp in place during casting.

Double droppers nab pompano, above, and whiting, below.

piece of brined clam strip, a Fishbites chunk and a piece of shrimp. The compression of this setup usually holds the bait package in place. When baiting hooks solely with shrimp, Gill wraps the bait with Ghost Cocoon thread—an ultra-thin, elasticized thread that binds soft baits to the hook without knots. Hook baits in the usual manner and then make several wraps with the thread along the entire length of the bait. No need to mummify the bait—you're just adding a brace to help it withstand the sudden shock of casting force. (This strategy works with clams, oysters, squid, or any soft bait.)

Gill stresses the importance of varying the baits on each of his double rigs (and among the different rods he sets), while also experimenting with accent beads. Noting the color of clam shells on a given beach helps him dial in the bead selection, while looking for patterns in his bites tells him

Baitfish migrations impact the fishing around Florida jetties and piers. More food equals more fishing opportunity.

what baits the fish prefer that day.

Baitfish movement plays a considerable role in surf dynamics, so pay attention to any food sources you spot in or near your surf zone. For example, when massive schools of menhaden mud northeastern beaches like those from Marine Land to St. Augustine Inlet, kingfish anglers move into the surf to castnet a day's supply of livies while sharks, cobia, tarpon and redfish move in to grab their morning meal.

Black drum are a common catch on Florida piers.

Similarly, the fall mullet run sparks a feeding frenzy that sees just about everything with an appetite chasing the southbound herds. When mullet run the beach, the real thing is hard to beat, but artificials like the D.O.A. Bait Buster, Koppers Live Target Mullet, Rapala Subwalk and MirrOl-ure MirrOmullet will also fool frenzied predators.

Other productive artificials include: spoons, Gotcha plugs, shallow runners like a Bomber Long A or Rapala X-Rap Slashbait, popping baits like the Cotton Cordell Pencil Popper or a Creek Chub Striper Strike and pilchard imitators like the MirrOlure MirrOdine or Live Target Scaled Sardine. Soft-body swimbaits with leadheads like Tsunami's Holographic Swim Shad, or jointed swimmers such as Sebile's Magic Swimmer and Storm's Kickin' Stick also earn a few looks.

Anglers can often reach the shallow edges of jetties from the shore and the rocks.

Walkin' and Lookin'

Wading the shallow surf blends the skills and tactics of hunting and fishing to locate and capture your target.

For those favoring a more active approach to the surf-fishing scene, ditching the stationary tactics and setting out on foot takes the game to the fish. Doing so means you'll trade the coverage and diversity of multi-rod spreads for the mobility and accuracy of individual casts. Either option can produce depending on what you're trying to accomplish.

D.O.A. Lures founder Mark Nichols wades the rock-littered shores from Hobe Sound Beach north to Fort Pierce, with snook and tarpon his primary targets. Handling big snook and even bigger tarpon at close range requires stout gear, so he'll use an 8-foot medium-heavy spinning outfit with 20- to 30-pound braid and 40-pound leaders for snook or 80-pound for tarpon. Stout tackle also helps him punch a bait through an onshore wind and fish with confidence around random rocks that a hooked fish always seems to find.

"I grew up in Texas where we would wade out into the surf, but here we're either standing on the sand or just calf-deep because we have larger waves than the Gulf of Mexico and a serious

Stalking the South Florida flats rewarded this angler with a permit.

trough right at your feet," Nichols said. "We catch lots of snook and lots of tarpon right in that first trough literally 15 feet away from the shore."

For snook and tarpon, Nichols throws his shallow running Baitbuster in calm water, but for most days, the heavier trolling model Baitbuster (line tie on top) works best in the active surf. Productive color patterns include black/silver, black/pearl and green/pearl produce well,

One rod and a few spare baits is all you need for a Florida surf wading mission.

For shallow casting pursuits, anglers must learn to work with prevailing conditions.

The combination of surf level and lure weight influences your presentation when working artificials in the wash.

but Nichols said the key is in the presentation.

"You can really stall the bait when you're fishing the trough," he said. "When you have some real surf, especially as it progresses into fall, if that water slides up on the beach, when it slides back, I can literally stall that lure right in that trough. I've had so many big snook right at my feet, I can just sit the bait right there in front of them when the water's going out."

Essential to surf wading, Nichols said, is learning how to fish in a strong current. Proper tackle is important, but so is the strategy of presentation and retrieve.

"When we get a hard wind, we can get a really hard rip current," Nichols said. "If it's ripping pretty hard and I'm trying to (control) something fairly light, I'll literally walk the current with the surf and try to stay in front of my bait.

"A lot of times, people can never get their baits down because of that current. There's that fine line between having too much weight where you end up snagging every time and not enough weight to get that lure down and keep it suspended in that turbid situation."

Nichols says spring finds huge jack crevalle of 20-plus pounds in the surf, while the cooler days of fall bring a notable uptick in Spanish mackerel action. He'll use a ¾- to 1-ounce CAL Jig with a 5 ½-inch CAL shad tail in white or chartreuse to reach these voracious feeders. Silver spoons are another mackerel charmer that also catch bluefish.

Shrimp imitators like D.O.A.'s original, Tsunami's Holographic Shrimp, or a Berkley Gulp! Shrimp on a light jighead will tempt snook, redfish, flounder, black drum and smaller tarpon in the surf, but Nichols suggests rigging the bait on a dropshot to optimize casting distance and to keep it off the bottom. (Dropshot: Tie your leader to the bait with a Palomar knot, leave the tag end about 24 inches long, pass the tag through the hook eye to position the bait perpendicular to the leader and then tie a ¼- to ½-ounce tear drop weight to the bottom.)

Rigging an artificial shrimp on a dropshot increases casting distance and elevates the bait presentation.

WadingTips

Match the hatch is always a wise principle for bait selection, but sometimes a literal application best suits the situation. Case in point: I watched an angler wade the surf off Stuart and eventually zero in on a large school of glass minnows swirling nervously in two feet of water. Predictably, several telltale pops bespoke the snook feeding below, but the typically productive shad-tail jig found no takers until a moment of simple brilliance. The angler picked up a dead glass minnow floating near the shoreline, stuck it on his jig hook and immediately found a taker. Lesson: when predators fixate on a particular food source, don't try to change their mind.

This angler sight casts for snook on Florida's Hobe Sound Beach.

Complementing the beaches with mainland access, secluded surf wading opportunities also exist throughout the various islands and glorified sandbars of eastern Biscayne Bay, where anchoring or beaching boats or kayaks in safe locations allows you to walk and fish as far as you'd like. Elliott Key (part of Biscayne National Park) offers

South Florida islands with or without mainland access make good wading spots.

several miles of wadable shoreline with good contour and deep water pulling in close at a couple of spots like Point Adelle (upper end).

The farther south you go, the greater the chances of spotting bonefish and permit. South Florida beaches see a lot of traffic, minimizing surf fishing opportunities. However, move south of the Miami beaches and you'll find that Virginia Key, Key Biscayne and Key Largo, along with several islands requiring boat access, offer waders plenty of shots at bones and permit. Bones like fresh shrimp on a light jighead or a No. 2 hook with a splitshot right above the knot. Permit are crab eaters, so keep a few in a flow-through bucket that you can tow down the beach. Fly fishermen find their crustacean patterns like the Merkin Crab or Borski Fur Shrimp well received in the South Florida shallows extending throughout the Florida Keys.

Throughout the coast, pay particular attention to any changes in shoreline contour (points, bends, depressions), as such features influence baitfish and predator positioning. Wading the beach side of a jetty can be productive but also take advantage of fish-attracting hard structures such as pier pilings, coastal bridges like Matanzas Inlet (south end of Anastasia Island), concrete and rock groins like those bracing the east shore of Virginia Key (north end of Biscayne Bay), the breakwaters of John U. Lloyd State Park (North Dania Beach), smaller rockpiles like those of Red Reef Park (Boca Raton) and larger scatterings like the namesake formations of Black Rock Beach (Talbot Island, north of Jacksonville). Minimize fatigue by keeping your

Any variance in shoreline contour, along with additional hard structure, signals fish-gathering areas worthy of extra attention.

WadingTips (cont'd)

Amelia Island Bait & Tackle
1925 S 14th St Ste 3
Fernandina Beach, FL 32034-4432
(904) 277-0775

Strike Zone
11702 Beach Blvd.
Jacksonville, FL 32246
(904) 641-2433

Fishin Shack
3514 S. Atlantic Ave.
Daytona Beach, FL 32118
(386) 788-2120

Billy Bones
10602 S Federal Hwy
Port St Lucie, FL 34952
(772) 335-3715

Capt. Harry's Fishing Supply
8501 NW 7th Avenue
Miami, FL 33150-2503
(800) 327-4088

Jacksonville Beach Pier
503 North 1st Street
Jacksonville Beach, FL 32250
Phone: (904) 241-1515

Canaveral Inlet Jetty Pier
400 Jetty Park Rd.
Cape Canaveral, FL 32920
(321) 783-7111

William O. Lockhart Pier
10 Ocean Blvd,
Lake Worth, FL 33460
(561) 582-3474

Juno Fishing Pier
772-1798 Ocean Dr.
Juno Beach, Florida 33408
(561) 799-0185

Deerfield Fishing Pier
200 Northeast 21st Avenue
Deerfield Beach, FL 33441
(954) 426-9206

tackle light. Lumbar packs—a more supportive version of the fanny pack concept—do well, as long as you remain shallower than waist-deep. Backpacks are one option, but shedding a pack and reaching for tackle risks spilling when you're standing in the water. Many anglers like chest packs but unless you use a rather small one, they can get in the way when leaning over and handling a fish. I use a Cabela's sling pack that hangs across neck and shoulder like a guitar and rotates from my back to a front position and then back out of the way without ever removing the pack. If you have faith in your lure selection and knot tying, a couple of spare baits in a Ziploc bag fit neatly in the chest pocket. (Add a chunk of cork or piece of soft-plastic bait to hook points to prevent poking.)

If you carry wading tackle in a backpack, be careful of spillage when opening over the water.

Accessible jetties are at:

- Fort Clinch jetties (North end of Amelia Island)
- Mayport Inlet (both sides)
- Boca Raton's south jetty
- Port Everglades south jetty (Dania Beach)

Shuffle and Shoo!

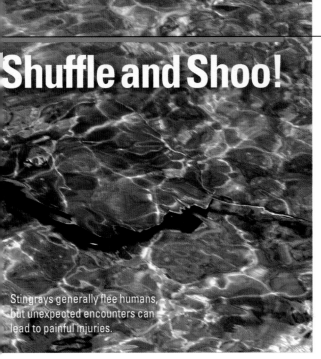

Stingrays generally flee humans, but unexpected encounters can lead to painful injuries.

A constant concern for wading and shore anglers in most Southern waters, various species of stingrays present a significant hazard when summer finds large numbers of these bottom skimmers gathering in the shallow surf for mating season. Contrary to common misbelief, the stingray's main defense—a venomous bony spike with inward slanted barbs—originates at the base of its tail, not the tip. When something like a human foot hits the animal, the tail flips forward and thrusts that wicked weapon toward the threat.

Like their shark cousins, stingrays are usually content to avoid human contact and even the giants with 6-foot wingspans will flutter away from your approach—that is, if they sense you in time. It's those rare instances when someone sneaks up on a snoozing ray, hops out of an anchored boat or kayak right above an undetected ray or dashes into the water and leaves the creature no time to flee. Just about all of these scenarios come down to wrong place-wrong time, but that's no comfort when you're headed to the ER with a miniature harpoon stuck in your foot.

Avoid such painful mishaps by traversing any warm-water wading scenario with the "stingray shuffle"—more of a gliding, sand displacing gait than the usual up-and-down step. The twofold advantage here is 1) Shooing away any ray within stepping distance and 2) Creating the noise, vibrations and drifting trail of sand/mud that alerts rays to your approach. (Also helpful with smalltooth sawfish; skates and guitarfish, both of which sport sharp dorsal spines; and electric eels that can deliver a mild, yet uncomfortable shock up to 37 volts.) The cownose (a.k.a. "bat ray") and spotted eagle ray also frequent coastal shallows, but these species spend most of their time swimming higher in the water column. These more mobile rays rarely come into contact with humans, but interacting with any wild rays under any circumstances creates a risky situation, so avoid contact whenever possible. If you catch a ray while fishing for other species, have a friend secure the tail or simply lay a damp towel across the barb, before attempting to dehook the fish. (Remember, the rays you feed and pet at Sea World and other marine parks have had their stingers removed for safety. Those in the wild are typically equipped to defend themselves.) In the event of any ray injury, seek beachside first aid to control bleeding and then proceed to a medical facility. Applying hot water to the site of the injury can ease the pain somewhat. Florida's Fish and Wildlife Conservation Commission recommends contacting the National Poison Control Center at 800-222-1222 for questions regarding stingray injuries.

Wading shoes are your first line of defense against stingrays and other hazards.

Shuffling your feet alerts resting stingrays to your approach and prevents unpleasant meetings.

Fall Jetty Blast

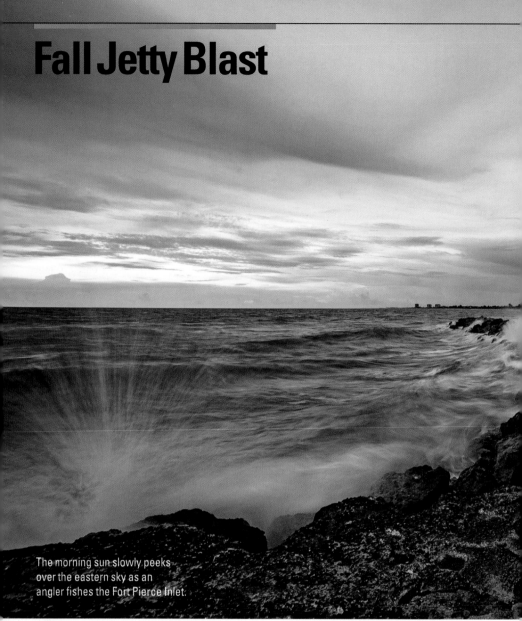

The morning sun slowly peeks over the eastern sky as an angler fishes the Fort Pierce Inlet.

Florida's Atlantic coast offers landbound anglers superb access to a bounty of surf species not only through its numerous fishing piers, but also several jetties that have been paved, partially-paved or otherwise surfaced for convenient foot traffic. Among them, Haulover Inlet's south jetty, Boynton Inlet's north jetty, Jupiter Inlet jetty/pier (south side), Fort Pierce Inlet jetty/pier (south side) and Sebastian Inlet's north jetty/pier bring a broad mix of species—flounder, mackerel, bluefish, cobia, sharks,

The fall mullet run brings incredible fishing action to Florida's east coast jetties as predators ambush the forage.

sheepshead and black drum—within easy reach.

For Capt. Chuck Rogers, one of the most exciting times to fish Florida's East Coast jetties is

During prime conditions of hard outgoing tides, anglers find it easier to fish from jetties than to fight the water from a boat.

the small and medium-size mullet into the inlets," Rogers said. "It's predominantly outgoing tide fishing and we normally do it on tarpon-style tackle or surf rods. It's easier to do this from land because that tide's ripping out of the inlet sometimes at 4 to 5 knots and you have a swell, which creates a giant wave right there, so it's hard to navigate a boat."

Rogers said he likes to keep his baits near bottom, but not on bottom. Expertise comes with experience (and the inevitable snag), but a fish finder rig with 1 ½- to 2-ounce weight allows him to bounce his weight off the rocks and walk it into the strike zone. Rigging with 30-pound braided main line, 60-pound fluorocarbon leader and a 5/0- to 6/0-heavy-gauge circle hook, Rogers will walk out toward the jetty's seaward end, make a long cast and then walk back in to keep his line straight. This facilitates a quick strike response so he can stick the fish and quickly work it up and away from the jetty rocks.

"Those fish are set up in that outflow and picking up baits," Rogers said. "Normally, it's mullet or pinfish for baits, but we have caught them on bucktails. Again, you have to be diligent with your movement because there are a lot of rocks in those inlets. Be prepared to lose some tackle."

during the fall mullet run. Oversized redfish are one of the top predators feeding on this buffet line and the action can become so intense, you'll need to show up early to stake out your position at popular inlets like Ponce, Sebastian and Fort Pierce, where working live baits with the tide is a good way to come face-to-face with a giant redfish, snook tarpon or jack crevalle. "In October through late-November, when the mullet run is happening, those big reds will follow

When the mullet run passes Florida's jetties, expect big redfish, like Alberto Knie's.

CHAPTER 14

Florida's Gulf Coast & Alabama

Throughout Florida's South to Central Gulf Coast, surf anglers will find plenty of mainland-connected beaches—from secluded gems like Marco Island, Sanibel Island, Anna Maria and Mullet Key; to perennial crowd pleasers like Naples, Englewood, Venice, St. Petersburg and Clearwater, where you'll rarely lack for company. Ferries shuttle anglers to free-standing favorites such as Cayo Costa, Egmont Key and Caladesi Island, while small boats or kayaks easily reach Three Rooker Bar, Anclote Key and North Bar (Tarpon Springs area); all with great surf fishing beaches.

Alabama offers excellent surf fishing on the barrier islands at the entrance to Mobile Bay: Gulf Shores, to the east, and Dauphin Island, to the west.

In this region, you'll find a seasonal blend of pompano, whiting, speckled trout, redfish, black drum and some large, menacing sharks.

While daytime shark catches are not uncommon, the action increases after sundown.

Gulf Grab Bag

In this region, you'll find a seasonal blend of pompano, whiting, speckled trout, redfish, black drum, flounder and jack crevalle that roam the bars, troughs and random beach structures like the rock jetty sprouting from Sarasota's Lido Key, the beach groins, piers and nearshore reefs along Bradenton Beach and the trio of breakwaters off Marco Island's southwest corner. When summer's post-spawn tarpon scatter along coastal beaches, a calm, clear morning may offer daybreak opportunities to float pass crabs under corks or cast 65M or 77M MirrOlures to well-known tarpon spots like Point of Rocks.

A limit of trout is not hard to come by for anglers wading Florida's Gulf Coast surf.

On the sand, jetties or piers, fishfinder rigs, double droppers and light Carolina rigs with shrimp, squid, cut sardines or sand fleas will deliver a mixed bag. With surf conditions generally much lower than those of Florida's east coast, Gulf rigs rarely need more than about 4 ounces of lead, but it never hurts to keep a few 6 and 8 ounces on standby.

Lighter surf also means Gulf beaches often present conditions more conducive to sight fishing for trout, reds, jacks—even cobia, barracuda and smaller sharks. During the summer snook spawn, live baiting off the deep island points can deliver trophy fish, but so might a quiet stroll down just about any Gulf beach where linesiders feeding in the first trough

On the sand, jetties or piers, fish finder rigs, double droppers and light Carolina rigs with shrimp, squid and other baits will deliver.

Summer finds snook scattered along Gulf beaches where they offer sight-fishing opportunity.

readily grab light jigs, bucktails, D.O.A. Shrimp, MirrOlure MirrOdines or other small, slow-sinking lures worked at a slight diagonal to the shore. Don't cast out too far, as the fish are usually in less than three feet of water. Also, don't be surprised to stick the occasional trout, redfish or flounder while strolling for snook.

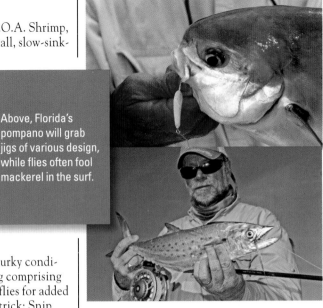

Above, Florida's pompano will grab jigs of various design, while flies often fool mackerel in the surf.

Pompano, although usually too erratic for sight fishing, will readily grab keel-weighted Doc's Goofy Jigs worked along the bottom. Vary your depth until you dial in a zone of consistency. In murky conditions, try a double pompano jig rig comprising Goofy Jigs with small pink teaser flies for added visibility. Another pompano surf trick: Snip the tail off a white or yellow grub, rig the body on a 1/8- to 3/16-ounce jig head, cast it into the surf and let it tumble forward to imitate a sand flea. (Berkley Gulp! Sand Fleas also work here.)

For plug casting fun with mackerel, bluefish, big reds and even cobia and tarpon, work a Heddon Super Spook Jr., Rapala Skitterwalk, MirrOlure She Dog or MirrOmullet in calm surf. In more active water, switch to a popping or chugging bait like the Creek Chub Striper Strike or jointed Knuckle-Head or the castable size 5¼-inch version of a Williamson Jet Popper. Subsurface presentations like a 3½-inch Bomber Suspending Badonk-A-Donk, Yo-Zuri Crystal Minnow or X-Rap Slashbait or Live Target's shallow running Spanish Sardine will also attract attention in the surf. When macks are thick, a Luhr-Jensen Krocodile spoon or a Gotcha affords the long casts and flashy presentations you'll need.

On the fly fishing scene, Sarasota's Capt. Rick Grassett prefers a 7- to 8-weight outfit with a clear intermediate sink tip fly line for most of what he finds on Gulf Coast beaches. The clear sink tip helps get the fly below any wave action in the surf. With snook, pompano, flounder, ladyfish, bluefish and Spanish mackerel the usual mix, Grassett uses his namesake Snook Minnow fly for linesiders and Ultra Hair Clouser flies for everything else. He ties his Clousers on long-shank hooks and leaves half of the hook shank exposed, as this stands up well to the toothy and rough mouths of mackerel, blues and ladyfish.

Anglers on the Sunshine Skyway Fishing Piers at the mouth of Tampa Bay have learned to entice grouper inhabiting nearby rubble piles by using an outgoing tide to drift their diving plugs out past the structures and then cranking the plugs across these artificial reefs. Here and on the two Fort Desoto piers to the west, mack-

Warm nights, stunning sunsets and lots of fish—that's the Florida surf appeal.

With Tampa Bay's Sunshine Skyway Bridge for a backdrop, anglers enjoy lots of surf zone action on the Skyway Fishing Piers.

Florida's Gulf Coast changes significantly from the Tampa Bay region to the Panhandle, but anglers find abundant action throughout the surf zone.

erel fishermen balance natural bait options with a specialized spoon rig comprising 2- to 4-ounce in-line sinker tied between braided main line and a 3- to 10-foot, 20-pound fluorocarbon leader (sized to experience level) with a size 0 or 1 spoon attached with a loop knot. When cast by swinging the rig under the pier and snapping it forward, the weight drops to the bottom and the spoon flutters higher in the water column.

Ingenuity also benefits Gulf Coast pier anglers seeking their share of the surf's tarpon and kingfish action. Freelined live baits quickly create chaos on a busy pier, so savvy anglers deploy an independent "outrigger" line anchored to the bottom and clip their live-baited fishing line to a sliding release clip affixed to the outrigger. When a big fish strikes, the bait pops free from the clip so the angler can fight the fish well away from neighboring lines.

Coastal Transition

North of Tarpon Springs, the coast abruptly transitions from sand and palms to mostly rock and salt marsh. This continues through the Nature Coast region, with hardly any publicly accessible shoreline fit for surf fishing except for a handful of isolated beaches such as Green Key (Port Richey), Hudson Beach (Skeleton Key, Hudson) and Pine Island Beach (south end of Pine Island, north of Bayport). Snook, redfish, trout, flounder, Spanish mackerel and the occasional cobia and tarpon are the likely mix for these areas.

After Pine Island, it's boats-only through most of the Big Bend, until a sweet little piece of shoreline pops out right below the St. Marks Lighthouse. Lighthouse Road runs through the St. Marks

A healthy trout population keeps upper Gulf anglers busy.

Wildlife Refuge and dead ends at a small parking lot facing the Gulf, just west of the light. It's an easy stroll down to the water where rocks, marsh grass, pier ruins, a long bar and proximity to the St. Marks River make this worth a stroll for mostly redfish, trout and flounder, although mackerel may run the deepwater edges when falling tides pull baitfish out the river.

Continuing westward, the surf access starts to increase with Bald Point State Park and the Alligator Point peninsula on the west side of Apalachee Bay, St. George Island and the Cape San Blas-St. Joseph Peninsula beaches. The sandy shores continue with St. Joe Beach, Mexico Beach, Crooked Island and Shell Island. Hopping over St. Andrew Bay, you find the

Northern Gulf beaches boast a distinctive look with sea oats sprouting from white dunes.

Surf tactics from Florida's Panhandle cross over naturally into Alabama waters.

famed Panhandle surf fishing beaches – long stretches of sugary white sand flanked by high dunes spanning Panama City Beach, Destin, Fort Walton Beach, Navarre and Pensacola.

Florida blends into Alabama at the west end of Perdido Key, with the same beautiful shoreline features continuing across Orange Beach, Gulf State Park, Gulf Shores and out to Mobile Point where Fort Morgan sits across from Fort Gaines at the mouth of Mobile Bay. Just off the bay's western edge, Dauphin Island adds a treasured coastal element with lots of angling appeal to draw surf fishermen across the namesake bridge. (A ferry dock at the east end links Dauphin to the northwest side of Fort Morgan State Park.)

Once you travel beyond the stronghold of the snook species, redfish gain prominence across Florida's Big Bend-Panhandle region.

Upper Gulf Bounty

ith the exception of snook pursuits, surf tackle and tactics vary little from Florida to Alabama. In fact, Mobile angler Mike Kennedy carries the same gear to Dauphin Island that he hauls eastward as far as Navarre Beach where deep water brings big sharks close to shore.

Other favorite spots include:

• West end of Dauphin Island where a jetty wall filling Katrina Cut (carved by the 2005 hurricane) attracts flounder, redfish, trout and sheepshead

• Fort Morgan Beach for big redfish, Spanish mackerel, bluefish and pompano

Redfish, above, and trout, below, roam the Northern Gulf's shallow surf.

• The beaches on either side of Perdido Pass yield a mixed bag, especially near the jetties

• Johnson Beach Recreation Area (east end of Perdido Key) has deep water close to beach bringing in a wealth of pompano, bluefish and big whiting.

Kennedy's typical surf setup includes one heavy-action 12-foot outfit with 30-pound braid and a fishfinder rig, a 9-foot medium-action rod with 20-pound line and a similar terminal rig and two 7-foot light-action spinning outfits with 15-pound braid and 10-feet of 20-pound fluorocarbon tied to a chicken rig (twin dropper loops with a 1- to 4-ounce pyramid sinker at the bottom). Fresh shrimp and sand fleas are the common baits for smaller surf species. Big reds like cut mullet or menhaden and if he's looking for big sharks, Kennedy fishes a live whiting on a 4-foot, 100- to 200-pound wire leader with a 12/0 circle hook.

Alabama surf fishing guide David Thornton splits his time between the beaches of Gulf Shores and the Alabama Gulf State Park Pier. On the latter, he'll fish live finger mullet on Carolina rigs for the flounder (a pier favorite) and look for the other surf regulars with double drop rigs baited with Gulf shrimp or the ghost shrimp that burrow into soft beach sand.

Northern Gulf pier anglers also find plenty of trout and redfish, while big cobia travel the surf zone and sand bar during their spring migration. Smaller fish return to the piers during late summer-fall, while kingfish often chase mullet and other baitfish across the longshore bar and drop into the deep trough where they can follow the food highway along the beach while remaining safe from big sharks outside the bar. Outrigger lines with live mullet or menhaden on wire rigs are the way to go for pier kings.

For the beaches, Thornton typically targets redfish, whiting, bluefish and pompano

The Alabama surf-fishing scene offers a productive mix of beach, pier and jetty action.

You'll find equal opportunity for heavy surf rods and medium spinning tackle on Northern Gulf beaches.

Diligent sand flea raking may turn up a day's supply of bait.

Above and at right, tranquil fishing awaits on many Northern Gulf beaches.

year-round, with speckled trout and Spanish mackerel favoring the warmer months. Shrimp on small Carolina rigs with ½-ounce weights and No. 2 to No. 4 hooks on 8-foot spinning outfits with 8- to 10-pound monofilament are the standard deal. For heftier fish like big reds, smaller sharks and tarpon, Thornton goes with a 12-foot outfit, 15- to 25-pound mono and a fishfinder rig with a 2- to 3-ounce pyramid sinker (6- to 8-ounce when it's rough). While waiting for a strike, 7-foot medium-action spinning outfits with 10-pound mono will handle most light duties with jigs, Berkley Gulp! Shrimp, spoons or topwaters for targets of opportunity like trout, mackerel and flounder.

An elevated view helps this Northern Gulf angler spot his sight-fishing targets.

Big Teeth, Big Danger

Specializing in after-hours beach action, Josh Ward heads up Shark Hookers, LLC.—a land-based, catch-and-release shark fishing charter team out of Naples. Target species include bull, lemon, blacktip, nurse, hammerhead, spinner, sandbar and tiger sharks. (Although rare, makos have been caught in the Florida surf and great whites have been sighted within casting distance.) Ward said that water temperatures and food source/supply determine optimal months, notwithstanding the annual tarpon congregations in Boca Grande Pass, which keep the bulls and giant hammerheads narrowly focused during May and June. Otherwise, here's the general lineup of species by the month:

March through early-May:
Bull, lemon, blacktip, nurse and spinner

Mid-May through September:
Bull, lemon, blacktip, nurse, hammerhead and tiger (hammerheads follow migrating tarpon; tigers are very rare, but possible)

August through October:
Blacktip, spinner and sandbar (prefer cooler water)

"If an angler is not targeting a specific species but just looking to catch a mixed bag, then the peak period is May-September," Ward said. "This is the time in southwest Florida when the water is warm enough and the sharks' food sources and supply are plentiful enough that there are not only a large number of sharks around, but the highest variety of species, as well."

South Florida shark anglers work to safely dehook a hammerhead for release.

The West Florida surf attracts a broad mix of shark species, with the greatest variety found from about mid-May through September.

Ward points to Marco Island, Sanibel Island, Barefoot Beach (Bonita Springs) and the beaches flanking Boca Grande Pass and Tampa Bay as prime spots. When selecting a shark fishing site, Ward looks for abundant prey (baitfish, stingrays) or indications that other predators like pelicans or dolphins have located the food. (Ward says dolphins and sharks commonly coexist, so don't believe the myth that the former intimidates the latter.) Dropoffs, submerged sandbars, and nearby passes or channels bode well for shark activity. Moving water is also important, as long as it does not impede proper bait positioning.

"Lastly, and this is just personal team preference, we look for beaches that are not heavily populated by people," Ward said. "We do not chum the waters or attract sharks to the beach, but perception is everything. Some people will see anglers fishing for sharks from the beach and assume the angler(s) are luring the sharks in, harming or killing the sharks and/or endangering the public. In order to protect our sport from public misconceptions that may threaten it altogether, we attempt to stay away from the public eye by fishing at night and/or at beaches with minimal human presence and human/water interaction."

Ward uses an array of mullet, stingray, mackerel, bonito, menhaden, and ladyfish—whichever matches the dominant local forage. Dead bait, he said, works best because you can't control where a live bait goes from the beach. You also can't control when the atfish show up and destroy softer baits like mackerel nd bonito. If the kitties are thick, he'll commit to he tougher stingray chunks. With any baits, soaking hem in a cooler half filled with sea water ensures naximum coverage of blood and oils on each piece. Contrary to some beliefs, big sharks do not require uge baits. Ward cuts his stingray bait into softball ze chunks and keeps his others to about 8 inches.

A typical shark setup employs two 9/0 Penn enators and one 12/0, both spooled with 0-pound Power Pro braid. The larger reel holds out 1,100 yards of braid with 400 yards of 100-pound Dacron backing, while one of the 9/0s holds 1,000 yards of all braid and the other packs about half and half braid-Dacron.

Custom-made leaders comprise 12 feet of 210-pound coated cable leader with a 16/0 or 20/0 circle hook matched to the bait and expected shark size. A 6- to 8-ounce pyramid weight slides along the leader, but Ward pegs it to maintain at least two feet of clearance to the hook.

"As a rule of thumb, the cable leader should always be at least two feet longer than the targeted shark," Ward said. "The extra length makes up for the amount of leader that could potentially be swallowed. That is important for not only successfully catching and landing the shark, but it also prevents the shark's tail from snapping the line and leaving a long leader hanging out of the shark's mouth."

When all goes as planned, Ward's 4-man team gets a good workout with a huge adrenaline rush, as subduing, reviving and safely releasing big sharks in the surf requires equal doses of skill, determination and disciplined focus. They've hauled some true monsters ashore but nothing has proven more surprising than the three goliath grouper, each over 200 pounds, that they've landed from the surf.

tingrays are a common food source r various sharks and a popular bait r surf anglers.

It's mostly a South Florida thing, but goliath grouper may grab baits intended for sharks.

Fighting & Landing Fish

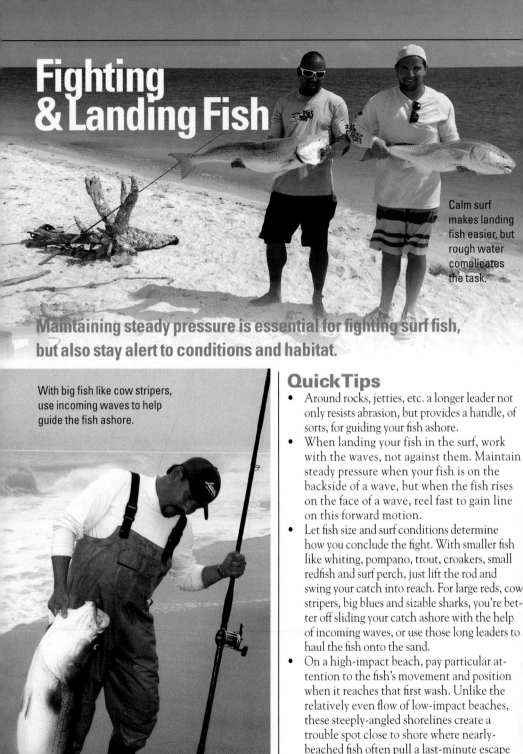

Calm surf makes landing fish easier, but rough water complicates the task.

Maintaining steady pressure is essential for fighting surf fish, but also stay alert to conditions and habitat.

With big fish like cow stripers, use incoming waves to help guide the fish ashore.

QuickTips

- Around rocks, jetties, etc. a longer leader not only resists abrasion, but provides a handle, of sorts, for guiding your fish ashore.
- When landing your fish in the surf, work with the waves, not against them. Maintain steady pressure when your fish is on the backside of a wave, but when the fish rises on the face of a wave, reel fast to gain line on this forward motion.
- Let fish size and surf conditions determine how you conclude the fight. With smaller fish like whiting, pompano, trout, croakers, small redfish and surf perch, just lift the rod and swing your catch into reach. For large reds, cow stripers, big blues and sizable sharks, you're better off sliding your catch ashore with the help of incoming waves, or use those long leaders to haul the fish onto the sand.
- On a high-impact beach, pay particular attention to the fish's movement and position when it reaches that first wash. Unlike the relatively even flow of low-impact beaches, these steeply-angled shorelines create a trouble spot close to shore where nearly-beached fish often pull a last-minute escape when the turbulent wash gives them just the right angle to spit the hook. Keep your rod tip high, maintain pressure and don't stop working the fish until it's completely ashore.

Hazards Include:

- Sharks chasing your hooked fish may come well inside your comfort zone.
- Focusing on your hooked fish, you may overlook stingrays, jellyfish, Portuguese Man-o-War, stumbling hazards, etc., so pay attention and maintain situational awareness.
- If you expect to enter the water to fight and land a fish, remove or secure all loose items from your pockets, waders, etc. Sneaky waves will confiscate unsecured items and that moment of lost concentration can cost you a fish.

Remove valuables from pockets before entering the water.

Piers & Jetties

Venice Fishing Pier
1600 Harbor Dr. South
Venice, FL 34285

Fort Desoto (Bay Pier & Gulf Pier)
3500 Pinellas Bayway
St Pete, FL 33715
(727) 864-3345

Redington Pier
17490 Gulf Blvd.
Redington Shores, FL 33708
(727) 391-9398

Big Pier 60
Pier 60, 1 Causeway Blvd.
Clearwater, FL 33767
(727) 462-6466

Okaloosa Island Fishing Pier
1030 Miracle Strip Pkwy. E.
Ft. Walton Beach, FL 32548
(850) 244-1023

Gulf State Park Pier
20800 East Beach Blvd
Gulf Shores, AL 36542
(251) 967-3474

Bait & Tackle Shops

Tall Tales Bait and Tackle
841 Vanderbilt Beach Road
Naples, FL 34108
(239) 325-8284

CB's Saltwater Outfitters
1249 Stickney Point Road
(Siesta Key, at Stickney Point Bridge)
Sarasota, Florida 34242
(941) 349-4400

Bett's Fishing Center
8926 126th Ave.
Largo, FL 33773
(727) 518-7637

Outcast Bait and Tackle
3520 Barrancas Ave.
Pensacola, FL 32507
(850) 457-1450

J&M Tackle, Inc.
25125 Canal Road
Orange Beach, Alabama 36561
(251) 981-5460

Accessible jetties are at:
- Venice Inlet (Venice, Fla.)
- North side of Pass-A-Grille (St. Petersburg Beach, Fla.)
- Johns Pass (Madeira Beach/Treasure Island, Fla.)
- Panama City Harbor Inlet (St. Andrews State Park)
- West side of Destin Inlet (Okaloosa Island, Fla.)
- Fort Gaines Jetties (Dauphin Island's east end)

CHAPTER 15

Texas to Mississippi

If for no other reason than the sheer coastline vastness, Texas offers the Gulf's greatest level of surf fishing opportunity. Separated by local cuts and major inlets like Galveston Bay, Freeport, Matagorda and Port Aransas, the Lone Star State presents a treasure trove of beaches with plenty of fish-attracting features. From Texas Point (west side of Sabine Pass), increasingly sandy beaches flank uninhabited marsh lands southwestward until you reach the lightly populated Bolivar Peninsula, which terminates at the north side of Galveston Bay.

Known for its wide open spaces, Texas offers surf anglers ample space to spread out and find their favorite Gulf species.

From beach casting for redfish, trout and whiting, to jetty fishing for tarpon and other large targets, the Lone Star coast offers diverse surf opportunities.

Lone Star Layout

From there, it's barrier islands all the way down to the Mexican border. Padre Island, with the Port Mansfield Land Cut dividing its North and South sections, dominates the coastal real estate with its majestic sand dunes and abundant wildlife complementing the beach habitat. Padre Island National Seashore spans 70 miles from Corpus Christi south to the Mansfield Cut and stands as the world's longest undeveloped barrier island.

Texas allows permitted beach driving in most areas, so reaching the distant sweet spots is just a matter of deciding how far you care to go. If you plan on travelling more than a few miles from a mainland access point, you'll want to do so in a 4-wheel drive vehicle, as some of these long, desolate stretches present challenging terrain. Avoid any trip-ending surprises by checking the weather and tide schedules before hitting the sand.

Surf anglers find productive fishing spots along the entire Texas coast, but a couple of key factors influence the big picture. South Texas guide Capt. Danno Wise, who fishes mostly from the Rio Grande River to the Mansfield Cut, said proximity of deep water to dry sand is most significant.

"Our first gut is a lot closer to shore than elsewhere (on the Texas Coast) and the 60-foot drop is a lot closer (within about 2 miles), so that allows larger fish to move in closer," Wise said. "Also, we generally get a lot cleaner water with better visibility and we have warmer currents for more of the year than in other areas. Also, we have fewer rivers and run-outs down here than they do (farther up the coast)."

Notwithstanding regional preferences, Wise noted that the species mix remains fairly consistent throughout the Texas Coast, with the exception of snook. During the warm season, Texans find loads of linesiders on the beach from the Brazos Santiago Pass on the southern end of South Padre to the Mansfield cut at the north end, as well as the Packery Channel, just south of Corpus Christi.

Speckled trout ran high on the target lis for anglers wadin the Texas sur

The Texas coast sprouts several prominent jetties providing anglers with deep water access.

Wading and Waiting

Throughout this region, redfish and speckled trout duel for shoreline superiority, with summers finding the speckled fish nudging ahead in the central to northern

Wading and casting topwaters or jigs is a good way to locate big Texas surf trout.

coastal areas. Topwaters like Heddon Super Spooks and MirrOlure Top Dogs, along with suspending baits like Paul Brown Originals account for plenty of nice trout, with a few redfish, jacks, mackerel and bluefish in the mix.

Daybreak with calm conditions can deliver fast-paced action with trout using the low light to chase baitfish within a few feet of shore. Darker colors are typically best early, with brighter patterns more effective once daylight increases. Surf guide Marcus Heflin throws topwaters, but he also likes the simplicity of a popping cork rig with a Berkley Gulp! Shrimp or a Swimming Mullet on a ¼-ounce jighead. Without the cork, he uses a 3/8-ounce head to maximize his casting

Low tide offers Texas surf anglers an opportunity to wade far from shore and locate trout around bait schools.

Soaking cut mullet or menhaden in the Texas surf often yields a big red drum encounter.

distance for trout and for sight casting to any flounder he spots during calm conditions.

Heflin targets beach points and flares in contours, which indicate good water action. He'll also walk out and "feel" the bottom with his feet to locate trenches, drop-offs or other features that may congregate forage and trout, along with whiting, redfish, black drum and pompano. Once he locates a promising area, he'll set out a spread of baits and wade for trout while others in his group watch the rods.

Seven-foot medium-action spinning rods will subdue most of the smaller surf species, plus they're easier for younger anglers to handle. Small pieces of cut shrimp will tempt everything he's targeting and Heflin likes to mix up his spread with Carolina rigs, fishfinders and double droppers with No. 1 or 2 hooks hung close to the main leader.

Bull reds are another favorite for the Texas Coast and Heflin finds them fond of cut mullet or menhaden fished on 12-foot heavy-action spinning outfits with 30-pound monofilament and 80-pound wire leaders. This setup, he said, will put the brakes on redfish up to 50 pounds, as well as the blacktip, bull, spinner and sand sharks he finds hunting the outer bars during spring and summer. (Tigers, great whites and thresher sharks make occasional surf appearances.) Rough water is ideal for big reds and shark action, but Heflin advises high caution, as riptides are common along Texas shores and anglers venturing out for a long cast can suddenly find themselves caught in the hazardous flow.

During lulls in the big rod action, Heflin may wade out as far as 50 yards off the beach on lower tides and walk parallel to the beach while scanning for bait schools that will attract trout. Just remember that you're not the only one looking for bait schools.

"Be careful what you wade to or you might end up in a school of feeding sharks," Heflin warns.

Texas jetties attract an assortment of species like mangrove snapper, below; but walk with caution on these hazardous structures.

Be Ready on the Jetty

Texans love their jetty fishing and the coast is blessed with several accessible and productive structures that bring anglers close to deep water opportunities. But risks balance the rewards. Tread carefully and maintain situational awareness at all times.

Watch the Water: What's dry and easy on low tide can turn into a briny beast when the incoming tide piles wave after wave against the structure you're trying to cross. Washes, where the sea flows through a low spot on the jetty, can be a death trap, so if you have to cross, time your crossing carefully. Existing current is challenging enough, but a piling wave can sweep you off the rocks and into the drink.

Don't Walk Alone: The buddy system isn't just for elementary school field trips. When life takes a turn for the dangerous, you'll want someone there to throw you a rope, help you back to your feet, or at least summon help.

Light the Way: Flashlights, headlamps or waterproof lanterns offer more than rigging convenience—they'll help you see where you're stepping after dark. Traversing jetties at night is a risky move not wisely undertaken by novices, but even those familiar with the scene lose the advantage when night falls. Adding reflective strips to clothing, hats, gear bags, etc. is a smart move that makes you easier to spot, should you require assistance during non-daylight hours.

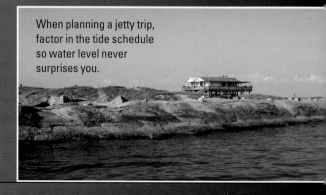

When planning a jetty trip, factor in the tide schedule so water level never surprises you.

Looking South

With calm surf and high visibility more common along the southern coast, sight fishermen often find superb conditions for stalking trout in the shallows. Despite this opportunity, Wise said these pursuits account for less of the day-to-day surf activity than in plug-casting strongholds like Galveston, Freeport, Surfside and Matagorda. Popular species for the South Texas surf include snook, pompano, black drum, sharks, Spanish mackerel and redfish.

"Occasionally, ling (cobia) will show up in the surf," Wise said. "Every now and then, bonito come in close enough to cast to. Late-spring through fall, we have tarpon that you can reach from the jetties, but during late-summer through early fall, they'll be within reach of dry sand as well."

For local jetty action, Wise suggests the Brazos Santiago Pass south jetty (access through Boca Chica Beach in Brownsville) and north jetty (south end of South Padre), along with the south Port Mansfield jetty (north end of South Padre). The latter sits several miles from the northern terminus of State Park Rd. 100, so you'll need a 4WD to reach this jetty. Same goes for the north Mansfield jetty (South

Look for incoming tides to bring Spanish mackerel close to Texas jetties.

Padre), as the long haul from where State Park Road 22 drops in south of the park office exemplifies the remoteness of some of these opportunities.

On these, and elsewhere along the coast, Wise suggests freelining live mullet for tarpon or casting a D.O.A. Deep Baitbuster or 1-ounce Blakemore Roadrunner on a 7-foot heavy action baitcast outfit with 20-pound braid and 60-pound fluorocarbon leader. The same baits will produce in the surf, but you'll want to step up to a longer rod for casting distance and fish-fighting angles. Fly casters armed with 12-weight rods will tempt 'poons with Haynes Pilchard flies and Bunny Strips on intermediate line.

For smaller tarpon—on piers or in the surf—Wise throws D.O.A. Shrimp and Baitbusters or bucktails on medium-heavy baitcasting gear and 15-pound braid. Snook like the same baits, along with live jumbo shrimp.

Jetty anglers also get plenty of shots at trout, redfish, sheepshead, black drum, flounder and bonito. Casting jigs, bucktails, shallow-running plugs and spoons will entice the more active predators,

Ballooning live baits off Texas jetties may reward you with a toothy kingfish.

Roy's Bait & Tackle Outfitters
7613 So Padre Island Dr
Corpus Christi, TX 78412
Phone: (361) 992-2960

Island Tackle
207 East Avenue E
Port Aransas, TX 78373
(361) 749-1744

Gaveston Bait & Tackle
9301 Broadway
Galveston, TX 77554
(409) 740-1185

Tyd's Bait and Tackle
24183 Hwy 1
Leeville, LA 70357
(985) 396-2676

Gorenflo's Tackle & Marina Store
119 Beach Blvd.
Biloxi, MS 39530
(228) 432-7387

Jim Simpson Sr. Memorial Fishing Pier
Hwy. 90 & Jeff Davis Ave.
Long Beach, Miss.

61st Street Pier
6101 Sea Wall Blvd.
Galveston, Texas
(409) 744-8365

San Clemente Pier
601 Avenida Victoria
San Clemente, CA 92672
(949) 492-113

Galveston Fishing Pier
9001 Seawall Blvd.
Galveston, TX 77551
(409) 974-4383

Bob Hall Pier
15820 Park Road 22
Corpus Christi, TX 78418
(361) 949-7437

while forage feeders like fresh shrimp or cut mullet on fishfinder rigs away from the rocks or knocker rigs close to the structure.

Late spring and summer see kingfish running close to South Texas jetties, where Wise finds ¾-ounce chrome Rat-L-Traps and big swimbaits productive. Ballooning a cigar minnow or ribbonfish on a wire rig will also make the reel scream.

Texas jetties attract a species mix meriting a wide array of natural and artificial baits.

Sheepshead are a favorite catch along the jetties and piers off the Texas coast.

Accessible jetties are at:
- Fourchon Beach, La. (East side of Belle Pass)
- Galveston East Beach Jetty, Texas (South side of Galveston Bay Channe
- Freeport Harbor Jetties, Texas
- Colorado River East Jetty, Texas (Matagorda Bay)
- Port Aransas Pass South Jetty, Texas (north end of Mustang Island)
- Packery Channel, Texas (Padre Island, south of Corpus Christi)

Delta Darlings

Louisiana's coast holds more than salt marsh. Sandy barrier islands are great for surf fishing.

Mississippi and Louisiana may not base their reputations on beach appeal, but respectable surf fishing opportunities certainly exist along their coastlines. Magnolia State anglers find stretches of mainland beach access from the towns of Waveland to Bay St. Luis on the west side of Pass Christian and the entire Gulfport-Biloxi shore, which includes the towns of Pass Christian and Long Beach. A handful of fishing structures like Waveland's Garfield Ladner Memorial Pier in Waveland avail a Mississippi Sound assortment including speckled trout, redfish, flounder, black drum, white trout, triple-tail and Spanish mackerel.

Also, the northwest tip of Deer Island is an easy run for small boats and kayaks and presents a long southern beach face, along with a set of rocky breakwaters off the northwest tip. Planted to protect Biloxi's casino strip, the emergent structures (some reachable on foot from Deer) are magnets for redfish, black drum and sheepshead.

For Mississippi's true surf fishing scene, visit the string of barrier islands (from the west)—Cat, Ship, Horn and Petit Bois sitting about 10 miles off the coast. All are reachable by private boats, while a ferry service docking at Gulfport runs to Ship's west end, just north of historic Fort Massachusetts. Surf targets include some of the redfish, trout, drum and flounder common to the sound side; along with whiting, pompano, larger sharks and bull reds.

Louisiana keeps a sweet set of surf fishing

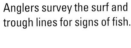

Anglers survey the surf and trough lines for signs of fish.

destinations hanging off its eastern coast. Here the uninhabited islands of the Breton National Wildlife Refuge (Chandeleurs, Curlew, Grand Gosier and the Bretons) offer some of the Gulf's finest redfish and speckled trout action. Accessible only by private boat, these tide-worn strips of sand and salt marsh see mostly wade fishing with topwaters, jigs and suspending baits, but flounder, black drum, Spanish mackerel, bluefish and sharks frequent these islands, so don't hesitate to stake out a few sand spikes and set a diverse spread of natural baits.

Moving westward, desolate barrier islands with low impact sandy beaches dotting the Delta perimeter offer an alternative to the endless marsh habitat. Pick a spot where you can cast with the wind and look for nearby passes and marsh drains to enhance the dynamics with current and additional food sources. Examples: the islands northeast of South Pass (just outside Garden Island Bay), both sides of East Bay (the notch between South and Southwest passes) and Bastian Island (north end of West Delta).

Grand Isle, the West Delta beauty with mainland access via LA 1 out of Port Fourchon, offers four miles of open beach with a pier at the north end, jetties at both ends and breakwaters spaced along the upper half. Trout are the top target in the surf, but you'll also find large redfish, flounder, mackerel and sharks here. Tarpon also frequent this area and occasionally come within range of surf rods soaking cut mullet or crabs.

Moving southwest from Grand Isle, Elmers Island and Fourchon Beach are the last sandy strips with mainland access before leaping across to Cameron Parrish. Here, in the region known as the "Cajun Riviera," spots like Holly Beach, Constance Beach and most any accessible point along Gulf Beach Hwy. (LA 82) offer inviting spots to set up the big rods for sharks and bull reds, or wade the waves and work topwaters and jigs for trout and smaller redfish.

CHAPTER 16

West Coast & Hawaii

With cool Pacific waters washing its coast, Southern California offers a vibrant and comfortable surf fishery through its northern boundary of San Luis Obispo County. Northern Cal anglers also find plenty of opportunity from beach, pier and jetty, but you'll see more shorts-and-T-shirt days in southern counties. Also, sandy beaches become scattered amid the northern coast's more rugged scenery, with its increasingly rocky complexion providing ample sunbathing spots for harbor seals and California sea lions. Kelp beds frequented by capricious sea otters are common throughout the coasts, so keep your casts close when these sea gardens abound or you'll snag every cast. As in most any fishing scenario, vegetation equals forage and forage attracts predators, so fishing kelp perimeters and open spots can prove productive.

From sun-drenched southern beaches to a more rugged northern end, there's no lack of surf-fishing opportunity along the California coast.

Jalama Beach in Santa Barbara County is known as one of the best perch fishing beaches on the west coast.

Surf Perch Shootout

Surf perch dominate the California coastal action, but diligent anglers find many other species.

Throughout the California coast, surf perch garner the majority of day-to-day angling attention. State waters hold walleye, calico, silver, striped, shiner, and redtail varieties, but the barred surf perch is most common. "Ninety-nine percent of the people who are surf fishing in Southern California are targeting barred surf perch and if they catch something else, it's a bonus," said local author and television personality Dan Hernandez. Hernandez looks for surf perch on long sandy beaches with lots of bottom features that offer feeding opportunities. Whenever possible, he suggests scouting the beach at low tide to find the cuts and depressions where surf perch will gather on rising water. In most cases, Hernandez prefers fishing incoming tides.

"As a rule, every time a wave hits the beach, it kicks out a sand crab or a ghost shrimp or a worm and that's

Top right, this big spotfin croaker ate a live sand crab in the California surf. Below right, a nice striped bass caught at Newport Beach, California.

why the perch are in there feeding," he said. "I know some people like fishing really low tides so they can cast farther out, but for me, I just think that a wave hitting fresh sand where it hasn't been in five or six hours seems to kick out more bait."

There's nothing wrong with choosing a promising area and setting out a spread of rods in sand spikes, but stroll the water's edge and you'll cover more water and eventually find concentrations of the schooling perch. A wading belt with a rod holder facilitates the dehooking and rigging/baiting duties by keeping both hands free, while a small pouch or box to hold a supply of baits allows

Walleye surf perch—a common California catch.

Find the fish-friendly beach features during low water and then target them when the tide rises.

The elusive ghost shrimp appeals to many of California's surf species.

leg," Hernandez said. "Sometimes, you'll catch them at the end of your rod tip."

Hernandez points to Sunset Beach, Long Beach, Seal Beach and Huntington Beach as good stretches for surf perch pursuits. Others include the sandy shores of San Clemente, Laguna Beach and Pismo Beach. Moving north, you'll find picturesque strips of sandy beach often tucked between coastal cliffs. Among them, look for surf fishing opportunities at conveniently accessible favorites like Carmel Beach, Monterey Bay and Half Moon Bay,

Surf perch often run in packs so if you catch one, stay put.

you to cover a broad area without frequently backtracking for more ammo.

"One tip I tell people is that if you find surf perch and you catch one, don't move – stay there," Hernandez said. "They're usually kind of balled up, so just stay in the same spot until you stop catching them and then start walking."

Hernandez prefers a light Carolina rig with a 1/4- to ¾-ounce weight, an 18-inch leader and either a No. 1 to 1/0 khale hook for live ghost shrimp, or a No. 6 to 8 baitholder hook for blood worms, sand crabs, or Berkley Gulp! crabs (small plastic grubs also work). Seven-foot, medium-action spinning outfits are plenty for the surf scene for two reasons: First, surf perch run about a pound each, with 2-pounders considered huge. Second, you just don't have to heave baits very far in the California surf.

"The fish are close—sometimes, you'll feel them hitting your feet or rubbing against your

Light tackle is usually sufficient for most California surf species.

as well as the more remote gems like those strewn along the Big Sur region. Reaching into California's upper end, you'll continue to find surf perch along sandy stretches. The Humboldt Bay area boasts some of this region's most consistent action, with long sandy beaches and jetties diversifying the offerings. Luffenholtz and Gold Bluff beaches also merit a visit.

Norm's Big Fish Tackle
1780 Pacific Coast Hwy
Seal Beach, CA 90740
562) 431-0723

Gus' Discount Tackle
3710 Balboa Street (at 38th Ave.)
San Francisco, CA 94121
415) 752-6197

Bittler Brother's Sport Center
355 SW Coast Hwy
Newport, OR 97365
541) 265-5300

Ed's Bait & Tackle
207 2nd Ave. SW
Iwaco, WA 98624
360) 642-2248

Nanko Fishing Supply
46-003 Alaloa St.
Kaneohe, HI
808) 247-0938

Ocean Beach Pier
5091 Niagara Ave.
San Diego, CA, 92167
619) 226-3474

Oceanside Pier
10 Oceanside Pier,
Oceanside, CA 92054
760) 722-3936

San Clemente Pier
601 Avenida Victoria
San Clemente, CA 92672
949) 492-113

Pismo Beach Pier
100 Pomeroy Ave.
Pismo Beach, CA 93449
805) 773-7034

Pacifica Pier
2100 Beach Blvd
Pacifica, CA 94044-2500
(650) 738-7381

Light Line Revolution

In the past, surf fisher and writer Bill Varney says, California surf anglers used much heavier equipment and tossed the bait as far from shore as possible. Today, they fish with ultra-light gear and catch some of the largest surf fish just feet from the sand. His book *Surf Fishing, The Light-Line Revolution*, explores the techniques, gear and locations of West Coast surf fishing in depth, with dozens of pictures and illustrations of all aspects of West Coast inshore surf fishing. Check out Bill's website at www. fishthesurf.com to find pictures of West Coast surf fish, tips, techniques, web cams and all the information you'll need to catch fish in the surf.

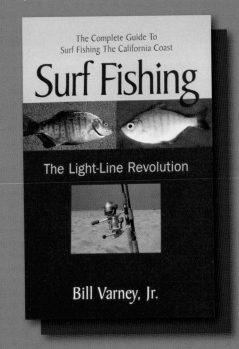

The Complete Guide To
Surf Fishing The California Coast

Surf Fishing

The Light-Line Revolution

Bill Varney, Jr.

Accessible jetties are at:
- Mission Bay Inlet (north of Ocean Beach, Calif.)
- Pillar Point Harbor (Half Moon Bay, Calif.)
- Reedsport jetties (both sides of the Umpqua River, Or.)
- Winchester Bay jetties just inside the Umpqua, Yaquina Bay Inlet (Newport, Or.)
- Grays Harbor (Westport, Wash.)
- La Push (Wash.) south jetty

Sporty little leopard sharks are abundant in the surf.

Other Opportunities

A chilly day on the beach produced a nice California halibut.

This tasty corbina adds to the surf mix.

Dan Hernandez notes that perch anglers fishing sandy beaches adjacent to rocky patches like Leo Carrillo Beach (north of Malibu) may also find a few California halibut. Smaller than the Pacific halibut of offshore waters, the local version runs about 5 to 10 pounds in the surf, so you'll want to upsize your tackle for targeted missions. Halibut will readily take natural baits such as ghost shrimp, anchovies and smelt, but hopping bucktails or swimbaits along the bottom is a good way to tempt the flatfish.

Striped bass, while occasionally caught as far south as San Diego, are more common to the central and upper regions. From the beach, pier or jetty, casting swimbaits, bucktails, spoons, shallow running plugs and poppers will draw the attention of nearby stripers. For a simple sand spike approach, bait a fishfinder rig with sand crab, clam, or smelt and let it soak in the surf.

Along the northern coast, rocky beaches—particularly those with nearby kelp beds—often find white bass of respectable proportions snapping at the same selection of baits and lures. Greenling—a smaller, yet sporty species common to the rock/kelp habitat—adds to the shore angler's options. Rarely growing larger than a pound, the greenling bites a variety of baits including cut pieces of sardine, anchovie, clams, mussels, shrimp, squid, worms and crab.

Corbina, a member of the croaker family valued for its fine table fare, is a common surf perch bycatch but certainly a species worth targeting. Try ghost shrimp, softshell sand crabs, blood worms, mussels or clams on a Carolina rig or small spoons for corbina, and other croakers (white, yellowfin, spotfin). And don't be surprised to find the leopard sharks (usually three feet or smaller) eager to intercept surf baits intended for someone in the perch or croaker clans. On the open beaches, fly fishermen find many of California's surf species willing to eat a variety of baitfish and crustacean patterns fished on an 8-weight outfit and intermediate line with a shooting head.

California pier and jetty fishermen also enjoy a mix of striped bass (central-northern coast), California halibut, larger leopard sharks, smoothhound sharks and shovelnose guitarfish around the perimeters, with cabezon, rockfish and monkeyface eels holding tight to the structure. Halibut and stripers will hit the same artificials and fishfinder baits they like off the beaches, while light knocker rigs with cut squid or shrimp will tempt the more homebody species. Leopards and guitarfish like anchovies, sand crabs and squid on fish finder rigs.

Pacific Northwest

This Pacific Coast campsite overlooks great surf fishing below.

Advancing northward into Oregon and Washington, rugged and rocky coastline, overlooked by the majestic Northern Pacific Coast Coniferous Forest, dominates the landscape. But along the way, surf anglers find several stretches of easy-access beaches, along with plenty of those isolated, get-your-hike-on pockets of sweet seclusion and rarely-fished surf.

Not far from Oregon's Coastal Highway 101, popular stretches of accessible sand include Harris Beach State Park, Whalehead Beach and Pistol River State Park at the south end; Florence and Washburne Beaches in the central region and Rockaway, Cannon and Seaside beaches to the north. Washington seems to hold its more accessible spots at either end of its coast, with several fishable spots, most with more challenging approaches, tucked in between. On the Columbia River's north bank, the Long Beach Peninsula begins a chain of beaches reaching up to Cape Elizabeth, where rocky cliffs and sporadic access to driftwood-strewn shores like Ruby Beach become the norm throughout most of the Upper Peninsula. At Washington's top end, coastal roads access Shi-Shi, Sooes and Hobuck beaches.

Surf perch gets top billing in the Pacific Northwest and the same tackle and tactics used in California water work here as well. Take note that the mass appeal of razor clam digs—throngs of shellfish fans stooping

California surf perch tactics also work for Washington and Oregon waters.

Tiny and tasty, the barred surf perch is a prized catch throughout the Pacific Northwest.

and digging through low-tide mud—should clue you in on a regionally popular bait option. Dig your own, or visit a coastal bait shop. Otherwise, ghost shrimp, blood worms or squid do just fine on light Carolina rigs. Beaches near the mouths of bays and coastal rivers like the Rogue River (Oregon), Columbia

River (Oregon/Washington border), Willapa Bay and Grays Harbor (both Washington), offer great opportunities to catch salmon—mostly Chinook and Coho (silver)—when these anadromous fish return to inland waterways for spawning. Chinook usually show up in July-August, with Coho arriving in late summer-early fall. Casting spoons and spinners or soaking cut herring on fish finder rigs can deliver red-hot action when the fish stage on beaches and feed up for their spawning runs. Along with the salmon, surf anglers may also find the smaller sea-run cutthroat trout, which spend more of their year in coastal shallows.

Fishing around this region's abundant coastal rocks and along with accessible jetties like those at Fort Stevens State Park (Tillamook Head at Oregon's northern tip) can yield a mix of flounder, halibut, kelp greenling, rockfish, cabezon and lingcod. Fishing ghost shrimp, squid, clam or cut herring on Carolina rigs, fishfinder rigs or dropshots will tempt a good mix of species, while hopping leadhead jigs with white curl tails over rocks is a good bet for rockfish, cabezon and lingcod.

Random sea stacks keep surf anglers company along the Oregon coast.

These bottom dwellers like to duck into rocky crevices when hooked, so stay sharp and react quickly. If a fish reaches cover and you can determine where he's holding, you might flush him out by "tickling"—carefully sticking your rod tip into the hole to prompt an exit. Conversely, because these fish spend a lot of time in such rocky refuges, don't hesitate to drop a baited hook right into the darkness. Here, of course, you're immediately disadvantaged, so quick response is a must.

Coastal rocks and various jetties add to the surf-fishing opportunity of the Pacific Northwest.

A variety of natural baits will tempt the common West Coast surf species.

Hawaii Tactics

Distinctive lateral coloration marks the yellowstripe goatfish—a common surf catch.

Blessed with incomparable beaches and warm, fertile waters, the Hawaiian Islands offer a colorful assortment of surf fishing opportunity. Leading the lineup, bonefish are commonly taken on shrimp, jigs and flies fished along sandy stretches, while strong currents swirling around rocky points and ledges of hardened lava formations bring great opportunity for anglers casting big poppers or fishing live goatfish or mullet on outrigger lines for white ulua (giant trevally) of 50-plus pounds. With deep water seldom far away, ulua and even tuna occasionally swing in close and give beach or rock anglers a good workout by grabbing spoons, diamond jigs, poppers and shallow running plugs. For the toothy crowd, chunks of bloody, oily bait on circle hooks and heavy wire leaders rarely go unnoticed by coastal sharks. Just be aware that sharks are venerated in Hawaiian culture, so if you actively target them do so respectfully and carefully release your catch.

Other common surf species include omilu (bluefin trevally), papio (juvenile ulua of 10 pounds or less), mamo (green damselfish), moano (manybar goatfish), weke (yellowstripe goatfish), pualu (yellow surgeonfish), ta'ape (blue stripe snapper), marepachi (soldier fish, or squirrelfish) and aweoweo (Hawaiian bigeye). Small fishfinder rigs or double dropper rigs baited with squid, shrimp or tako (octopus) will handle most of the smaller surf/reef species, while jigs with curl tails and topwater poppers are a good bet for papio and smaller ulua.

Ask nicely and locals might point you to particularly productive beaches throughout the eight "main islands" or some remote slice of angling paradise farther up the chain.

Regardless, Tab Terayama of Nanko Fishing Supply in Kaneohe (southeastern O'ahu) offers some encouraging advice: "People ask me all the time, 'Where's the best place to go fishing?' and I tell them, 'You can practically fish the entire

island shores.' Just look for beaches with deep water or channels nearby. You can even walk out on low tide and plug the edge of the reefs for papio and ulua."

Wading Hawaii's shoreline shallows, like the Paiko flats near Honolulu, can yield bonefish action.

Steve Wozniak (not the Apple guy) pictured on these pages has fished in 79 countries and counting. In July, 2010 he reached a lifetime goal of catching 1000 different species. As he marches to the 2000-species mark, you can read his blog at 1000fish.wordpress.com. Eels are part of Hawaii surf fishing, he says, like it or not.

Keep it Simple, Keep it Fun

Sometimes, simple is best. Good example— "poke poling" the crevices, crannies and hidey holes amid California's rock jetties laid bare by outgoing tides. When the water recedes, small pools remain within the solid structures and resident fish that roam the rocks tuck themselves into these low-tide holding cells until the incoming cycle renews their habitat. Species such as cabezon, rockfish and monkeyface eels grow hungry as they await the tide's return and anything edible that falls into their pool usually meets with aggressive response.

Jetty anglers can fill the generally less productive low-tide period by snooping along the rocky structure and "poke poling" their way to a few extra keepers. The same surf rods you'll use for traditional jetty fishing will work, but a shorter outfit like the 7-footers common for surf perch efforts is more manageable and enables you to get closer to the holes for better presentations and quicker reaction. Conversely, if the fish seem spooky, using that longer surf rod (or a sturdy 10-foot bamboo pole) affords the stealth advantage of distant presentations.

Tie your main line straight to a 2/0-3/0 straight shank hook and bait it with squid. (Threading the bait on the hook extends its use.) Drop the rig straight into holes with a short line and yank out whatever bites. Watch your line and when the slack disappears, you have a bite.

Hawaii's surf fishing scene has a similar tactic that's more of an "old-school" traditional method for catching small, but tasty species like moi (threadfin) and aholehole (flagtail). Using long bamboo poles with line tied straight to the tip, island anglers stroll across lava rocks and dip their hooks baited with squid or shrimp into holes and tidal pockets amid the dark structure. Another old-school version of this "pole fishing" targets oama (juvenile goatfish) or halalu (bigeye scad). Folks often gather in small groups to wade placid shores and gather a bunch of these small fish to fry and eat whole. Some use oama as bait for papio and ulua (trevally).

Crustacean Capture

Yearning for a fresh crab dinner? Snares offer an interesting option, but always check local regulations.

Crab snaring success requires a lot of trial and error, but experience will help you dial in the details.

If you think California's jetty and pier fishermen are crabby, you're not too far off base. But that's a good thing—especially for those who enjoy crustacean dinners. Tasty Dungeness and red crabs common around most hard structures occasionally clamp a claw onto baited hooks intended for finfish, but those intentionally fishing for crabs employ a clever device generally known as a "crab snare."

Designs vary, but the general concept starts with a corrosion-resistant wire bait cage with a bottom weight and monofilament snare loops secured to the frame with crimped ends. When crabs approach to sample the bait, a claw or leg usually ends up inside one of the loops. As you retrieve the snare by hand line or on a stout surf rod, the forward movement tightens the loop against the crab's resistance, thereby snaring the critter

for a quick trip to the surface.

Short of employing an underwater camera system, this is a game of trial and error. Experienced anglers who've dialed in productive areas soon develop a feel for how long to soak their snares. Impatience is the novice's detriment, as yanking your snare too soon spooks uncommitted crustaceans and lessons the likelihood of a second

Crab snares rely on multiple loops, which tighten on claws or legs when retrieved.

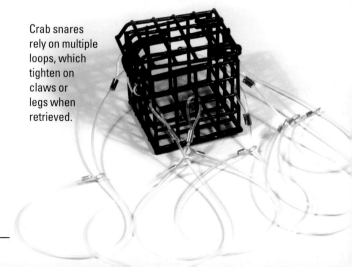

This angler pulled a nice Dungeness crab from the west coast surf with the aid of a snare.

chance on that particular spot. Also, when checking your snare, a steady and moderate pace proves more efficient than sudden, erratic jerking.

Best bet is to set your snare, pick up a fishing rod and keep yourself occupied while you allow time for crabs to take interest. Start with a 10-minute soak, evaluate your results and incrementally back down on the time until you find the right balance of patience and productivity. A slow day might give you fewer individual soaks, but if the area's crawling

A crab caliper will help keep you in compliance with size regulations.

(pun intended) with crabs, you'll need to speed things up to maximize your opportunities. In California, or any state with coastal crabs, check local regulations for size, season, bag limits and regional snaring restrictions; and keep a crab caliper (South-bend.com) handy to check each crab for legal size. Crab snares are easily to make, but you'll find them at local tackle shops and online retailers. Eagleclaw.com offers a 6-loop model, but check for regulation compliance. States may limit number of loops.

CHAPTER 17

Conservation & Advocacy

Throughout 16 chapters, we've presented surf fishing as an activity of easy access and low commitment. You walk to the ocean; you walk away from the ocean. Just don't walk away and forget about this magnificent resource and the issues affecting its shoreward fringe.

Legislation may impact beach access. Fisheries management decisions can have long-term implications for surf fishermen. Familiarize yourself with these matters affecting your sport. Let your voice be heard throughout the resource management process. Support conservation/advocacy groups that fight for healthy fisheries and your right to enjoy them.

Habitat protection initiatives have drastically reduced access to popular surf fishing areas like Cape Hatteras National Seashore Recreational Area.

Limited access to beaches, above, may deprive anglers of surf catches like pompano, right.

Upcoming Threats

Misdirected concerns over lead hazards for waterfowl could threaten the production of common surf-fishing weights.

The American Sport Fishing Association (ASAFishing.org), local fishing clubs and your state chapter of the Coastal Conservation Association can provide information regarding current issues that affect surf fishermen. ASA's KeepAmericaFishing.org provides a hub for angler advocacy opportunities, news alerts and campaign contributions. Each year brings new threats:

No Fishing Zones

Marine Protected Areas (a.k.a. No-Fishing Zones) prohibit angling activity for the ostensible purpose of rebuilding fisheries. From Southern California to the Florida Keys, a number of these closures have been proposed and in some cases implemented. Little evidence supports their effectiveness, and many viable alternatives exist. Remember, the tax-paying public owns the resources, so let your state and national legislators know your opinion on such matters. Preventing closures is a tough battle, but not nearly as tough as trying to reverse such actions.

Inshore Netting

Large, non-selective nets set by commercial fishermen are devastating to coastal fisheries. Today, most states prohibit gill nets in inshore waters, but commercial interests continue to mount numerous challenges to laws such as Florida's 1994 constitutional net-restriction amendment. Recreational anglers owe it the resources they enjoy to keep diligent watch for illegal netting and to support the efforts of state and national organizations like the Coastal Conservation Association (JoinCCA.org), which continue the fight against such threats.

Baitfish Management

As the prey goes, so goes the predator. In other words, take away the baitfish and many of

True appreciation for the sea's vast resources is reflected in one's commitment to environmental stewardship.

the sport fish species that surf anglers pursue will decline. Example: Commercial fishing pressure has caused a significant population decline among Atlantic menhaden—an important food source for red drum, bluefish and striped bass. Menhaden hold high commercial value. Factories process their oil and render the fish into animal feed and other products. But the fish are far more valuable as a vital link in the marine food chain. Protecting menhaden from overfishing will greatly benefit several surf-fish species.

Lead Weights

Concerns over potential mortality among waterfowl that ingest lead fishing tackle has prompted the imposition of bans on the sale and/or use of lead fishing tackle in several states and on National Park Service Lands. Certain conservation groups have also pushed for a federal ban on all lead fishing tackle. Mandatory transitioning to non-lead fishing tackle would require significant and costly changes for manufacturers and anglers. Surf anglers will want to keep an eye on this issue.

Regulations for Offshore Fish

Pier and jetty fishermen occasionally catch fish traditionally considered offshore species—among them, gag grouper and mangrove snapper throughout Florida and the Gulf of Mexico, tautog in the Northeast and lingcod along the Pacific Northwest. Therefore, it's important for surf anglers to stay abreast of all relevant fisheries regulations.

Beach Renourishment

Popular tourism towns strive to maintain the

beaches that bring the visitors by adding sand—often non-native materials—to replace what the sea constantly claims. This wouldn't be such a bad deal if all that filler stayed put, but it often does not. Regular wave action gnaws away beaches, but one strong storm is all it takes to wash the majority of the renourished beach into the ocean where

Despite municipal efforts to rebuild eroded beaches, the sea's relentless gnawing often claims the new fill material.

it usually settles over nearshore reefs. Often the renourishing material is of a larger grain than the fine grains formed through years of pulverizing surf. Such dense beach material is often devoid of mole crabs and other beach forage that cannot burrow into it. Even worse, perhaps, is unnaturally fine-grained, fill material which clouds the waters.

Storm Recovery

When extreme weather events destroy piers, erode popular beaches and otherwise limit surf-fishing access, the angling community is often the driving force in prompting and assisting reconstruction efforts. Remember, your fishing-related purchases generate significant tax dollars, a portion of which should support the activities responsible for generating this revenue.

Environmental Stewardship

Local fishing clubs and conservation groups usually schedule at least one beach cleanup day a year. If you can't find any organized efforts, grab a trash bag and leave the beach better than you found it.

Habitat Restoration

Inshore environments, particularly estuaries, provide the nursery habitat necessary for most coastal sport fish species, while also functioning as a food production facility that cranks out endless supplies of crustacean and baitfish forage. Environmental groups such as Tampa Baywatch on Florida's Gulf Coast offer anglers opportunities to participate in restoration efforts such as seagrass planting, oyster reef installation, invasive plant removal, coastal cleanups and monofilament recycling. Financial support also helps these programs continue.

Release Right

Each time you send a fish back to the surf for size, season, bag limit or catch-and-release preference, make sure your catch returns home in good condition. That starts with careful handling. Avoid touching the eyes and gills and avoid rubbing away the protective slime coat. Minimize the time your fish is out of water by making sure your fishing pal is ready to snap that trophy shot as soon as you secure the fish. For larger catches—big stripers, redfish, black drum, sharks—walk the fish through the shallows and support it with one hand under the tail and one under the belly until the fish recharges its batteries.

Outreach and Mentorship

Encouraging others to fish the surf and providing an appropriate level of teaching and assistance broadens the sport's participation and fosters more of all that good stuff we talked about in Chapter 1. Family members, friends, the guy across the street—invite someone to join your next surf-fishing trip. You'll quickly see how cool it is to pass along what you've learned. And if you ever need a reminder of what's most important in life, volunteer to help with a surf fishing derby for underprivileged or special needs kids. Again, local fishing clubs are usually your best source for such opportunities, or at least information on larger state and regional programs.

Presenting technical instruction with a patient, encouraging tone helps create a learning environment for beginners.

Beach Access

Surf anglers concerned about access issues may consider supporting local and national advocacy groups.

At times, reaching the ocean can prove more challenging than catching fish, as surf anglers find their desired beach closed for various reasons. One well-publicized access issue has been that of Cape Hatteras National Seashore Recreational Area (CHNSRA), where the National Park Service's Off-Road Vehicle management plan closed vast areas of shore to public use and greatly limited ORV access. The intent was to limit environmental impact to sand dunes where various seabirds and turtles nest.

Opponents argue that the plan imposes restrictions exceeding what's needed for adequate environmental protection, while impacting local economies, which depend on tourism and recreation. Angler access advocacy comes from groups such as the North Carolina Beach Buggy Association (ncbba-online.com) and the American Sportfishing Association (ASAFishing.org).

Elsewhere, New Jersey has a history of limiting beach access through direct property rights claims of oceanfront property owners and indirect efforts such as costly beach badges, limited parking, lack of restrooms and bans on food and beverages. In Florida, several communities have faced controversial debates over public access rights to beaches adjacent to private oceanfront properties where tax dollars paid for renourishment projects.

A key proponent of public access, the Surfrider Foundation is an environmental organization dedicated to the protection and enjoyment of the world's oceans, waves and beaches for all people through conservation, activism, research and education. The foundation promotes the rights of all recreational user grouper to enjoy low-impact beach access and encourages the public to work cooperatively with local residents and decision-makers to ensure maximized coastal access for all. For information, visit Surfrider.org.

Other advocates for fishing access include:

- Coastal Conservation Association (JoinCCA.org)
- Long Island Beach Buggy Association (brickworxclub.com)
- Long Island Beach Access Group (www.LIBAG.org)
- New Jersey Beach Buggy Association (NJBBA.org)
- Assateague Mobile Sportfishermen's Association (keepersofthebeach.com)

A New Cast to Angling Action

For many anglers, sight fishing the Florida surf conjures images of still, warm days and flat, gin clear water. In the southern half of Florida, snook might be the most commonly sight-fished species along the sandy beaches of the Atlantic, Gulf of Mexico and the many bays and rivers that pock each shoreline.

Like snook, many shallow water predator species are known to have very keen eyesight, yet anglers are able to fool them with artificial lures which sometimes only very generally resemble something alive. While this seems like it doesn't make any sense, a quick explanation of basic eye structure of most fish can help explain the paradox.

As is the case with many vertebrate animals, fish eyes typically contain a layer called the tapete lucidum, a thin reflective layer behind the retinae that improves night vision. This structure is responsible for the reflection seen when lights shine on cats, raccoons, gators and a host of other animals. In the case of snook, this well-developed structure is partly responsible for their night time feeding habits, as well as the insomnia of many snook anglers.

While it provides a fantastic night vision advantage, scientists believe that in instances of intense light it actually blurs vision, or creates double vision. For this reason, when targeting snook during the brightest of days, anglers who focus on making sure their lures are close in size and color to the local bait runs—and facilitate proper lure action—can achieve more success than those who focus only on visual details of the lure itself.

In the case of snook, surf fishing is generally a summer game and many anglers know that these snook are hungry because they are involved in the summer spawning activity that takes place at or near inlets and river mouths. The very predictable spawn sessions of snook make them particularly vulnerable, especially when factored in with their intolerance of cold water (as evidenced by the fish kill during the chilly 2010 winter).

However, even within the clouds of hypothermic winter fronts there can be a silver lining. One direct result of that deadly 2010 Florida winter was the development of the Angler Action Program (AAP) by the Snook & Gamefish Foundation. The AAP is a recreational fishing database where we everyday anglers have the opportunity to share our fishing data for the purpose of better fishery management (as well as building a personal and private fishing log).

After only three years of data collection, your snook angling buddies contributed data that was used directly by the State of Florida in their 2011 snook stock assessment, then again in the 2012 stock update. This is the very first time recreational data has been used at the state level in the United States. Maybe coincidentally, 2012 was also the very first time snook met the state's spawning potential ratio goal of 40 percent.

Today the AAP covers all species of fish caught anywhere in America. So, for the first time in a long time anglers can work together on a huge project that allows us many opportunities, from assisting with better fishery management to demonstrating that we are willing and able participants of providing a better fishery for ourselves and our children. The AAP is also now being used to quantify habitat restoration and rehabilitation efforts, which will help raise funds for future projects as well as identify and protect critical habitats. Learn more at www.angleraction.org, or download the free iAngler app from your smartphone store.

— *Brett Fitzgerald*

Catch data collected through the Snook & Gamefish Foundation's Angler Action Program provides valuable insight for fisheries management.

INDEX

INDEX

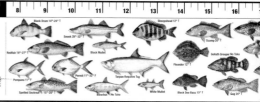

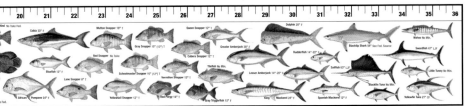

SURF FISHING DVD

The *Sportsman's Best: Surf Fishing* DVD brings the pages of the accompanying book to life. Join author David A. Brown and some of the best known experts on surf fishing as they explain the process of site selection, choosing tackle and learning the skills needed to catch fish from shore.

DVD CHAPTERS:

- ▶ **THE APPEAL**
- ▶ **NATURE OF THE SPORT**
- ▶ **TACKLE OPTIONS**
- ▶ **APPAREL**
- ▶ **TOOLS AND TECHNIQUES**
- ▶ **GEAR FOR CATCHING AND KEEPING**
- ▶ **BAIT RIGS**
- ▶ **ARTIFICIAL RIGS**
- ▶ **REGIONAL ROUNDUP**

SPORTSMAN'S BEST

SURF FISHING

With easy access and great opportunities year-round, surf fishing just might be your best fishing option. Read this book, watch the DVD, the rest is up to you.

"If you're looking to fish from a beach, jetty, or pier, this book and DVD are worth checking out. After reading the book and watching the DVD, I'm sure you'll be heading out to the surf with rods in hand."

—*Blair Wickstrom,*
Publisher,
Florida Sportsman

DVD Executive Producers: Chris Collins & Scott Sanders